Discovering ART

Sculpture

Stuart A. Kallen

ReferencePoint
Press®

San Diego, CA

About the Author

Stuart A. Kallen is the author of more than 250 nonfiction books for children and young adults. He has written on topics ranging from the theory of relativity to the history of rock and roll. In addition, Kallen has written award-winning children's videos and television scripts. In his spare time he is a singer/songwriter/guitarist in San Diego.

© 2015 ReferencePoint Press, Inc.
Printed in the United States

For more information, contact:
ReferencePoint Press, Inc.
PO Box 27779
San Diego, CA 92198
www.ReferencePointPress.com

LIBRARY OF CONGRESS CATALOGING-IN-PUBLICATION DATA

Kallen, Stuart A., 1955–
  Sculpture / by Stuart A. Kallen.
    pages cm. — (Discovering art)
  Includes bibliographical references and index.
  ISBN-13: 978-1-60152-678-6 (hardback)
  ISBN-10: 1-60152-678-4 (hardback)
  1. Sculpture—Juvenile literature. I. Title.
  NB1143.K35 2014
  730—dc23
                                                2013049192

Contents

What Is the Art of Sculpture?

Sculpture can elicit strong emotions in a viewer, tell a compelling story, or forever preserve a sculptor's vision. Sculpting is an artistic process that involves patience, determination, and occasionally, brute strength. Unlike a painter who applies paint to a canvas with a few brushes, sculptors work with heavy clay, large chunks of stone, red-hot bronze, or even large pieces of trash. These materials might be cut, carved, hammered, scraped, sanded, burned, or baked.

Whether a sculpture is bronze, marble, wood, clay, bone, or assembled from everyday objects, it is made from materials that are humanized by the artist. Formless blocks of stone, clay, or metal become recognizable forms that can inspire joy, sorrow, fury, fright, astonishment, and awe.

Lion Man

Around thirty-two thousand years ago, people on the European continent created the first known sculptures from clay, wood, stone, and ivory. The oldest known sculpture, referred to as Lion Man, was created around 30,000 BCE and was discovered in Germany in 1939. Lion Man features the head and body of a lion combined with the upright posture and two-legged stance of a human. The sculpture was carved from an ivory mammoth tusk using a flint knife. That makes the work a subtractive sculpture, meaning that whoever made it carefully removed, or subtracted, material through cutting, chiseling, scraping, and chipping.

Like most ancient sculptures, Lion Man was not carved with the specific intent of creating a beautiful object; it had magical or religious significance. Lion Man was likely an important talisman meant to provide hunters with the strength and hunting skills of a lion. But Lion Man is beautiful and represents one of the earliest examples of creative inspiration. As art reviewer Martin Bailey explains: "What was striking about the sculptor of the *Lion Man* is that he or she had a mind capable of imagination rather than simply representing real forms."[1]

Casting Bronze

While subtractive sculptures are some of the oldest, artists in China and India perfected another type of sculpture technique around 3,000 BCE. Bronze casting is a complex, multipart process that first requires a sculptor to make a mold in the shape of a sculpture. A mixture of copper and tin is heated to a very high temperature to create liquid bronze, which is poured into the mold. When the metal cools and hardens, the mold is removed, leaving a cast-bronze sculpture.

By the seventh century BCE, the Greeks were using molds and metal casting to produce thousands of bronze statues, many of which are on display today in museums around the world. In addition to perfecting the process of bronze casting, the Greeks also added an influential artistic element to their sculptures. Greek artists featured realistic-looking figures of young, athletic males and full-bodied female nudes.

> **Words in Context**
> *subtractive*
> A type of sculpture in which material has been subtracted through carving, chiseling, cutting, and rubbing.

The Divine One

While the Greeks perfected sculpture, the Romans gave this art form its name. The word *sculpture* originated around three thousand years ago in Rome and was originally used to describe sculptures carved from granite, marble, and other stones. In Latin *sculptura* means "to carve or cut out of stone." Some of the most well-known sculptures in the world are carved from marble, including Michelangelo's huge masterpiece *David*, created in 1504 during the Italian Renaissance.

Renaissance philosophers believed that sculptures of unparalleled beauty were the result of divine inspiration. Among the sculptures included in this group is Michelangelo's *David*, carved from marble and completed in 1504. A close-up view of the head of David is pictured.

By the time Michelangelo carved *David*, Renaissance philosophers believed that great sculptures were the result of divine inspiration, a sort of frenzied creative spirit handed down from God. This inspiration allowed artists to produce works of unparalleled beauty.

Because of his perceived God-given artistic powers, Michelangelo was known as *Il Divinio*, or "the Divine One." It was believed that anyone who gazed upon the sublime beauty of *David* and other Michelangelo works would be affected by the artist's godlike powers and be transported to a higher plane of spiritual existence. While few sculptors equaled Michelangelo, the standards he set concerning beauty, spirituality, and inspiration were imitated by countless others and continued to define the art of sculpture until the nineteenth century.

Challenging Concepts of Art

In the 1910s sculptors began to challenge the artistic standards handed down since the Renaissance while expanding the types of materials used in sculpture. In 1913 Spanish artist Pablo Picasso created the first assemblage sculptures. These were not cast or carved but assembled out of separate elements. Picasso worked with sheet metal, bottles, wire, cans, and discarded items he found on street corners.

In 1915 French artist Marcel Duchamp took Picasso's concept one step further and created another genre of sculpture, the readymade. Rather than assemble everyday items into a sculpture, Duchamp simply purchased products such as a snow shovel and a urinal and displayed them as art. Readymades called into question basic concepts about sculpture, making a statement that anything can be a sculpture if the artist says it is.

From the prehistoric era through the Renaissance and into the modern age, sculptures have presented art in three dimensions: They have height, width, and depth. But concepts of sculpture have changed and evolved over time. From clay and stone to trash and toilets, sculptures represent more than the materials used in the making. Sculptures can inspire and stimulate as well as confront, dare, and dispute. And they symbolize artistic concepts as unlimited as the human imagination.

Chapter One

Bringing Clay to Life

Clay has long been one of the most useful substances known to humankind. A natural product of the earth, clay is extremely malleable and can be easily shaped into cups, water jugs, bricks—and works of art. When exposed to fire, clay hardens into durable forms known as ceramics. Some of the oldest known human-created objects in the world are ceramic goddess sculptures, including the Venus of Dolní Věstonice, discovered in Brno in the Czech Republic. This is a 4.4-inch (11 cm) figurine, believed to be a female fertility goddess. The sculpture was made around 29,000 BCE. The Venus of Dolní Věstonice is known as an additive sculpture. The term refers to the fact that the artist creates the sculpture by adding more material to it. Whoever made the Venus of Dolní Věstonice started with a lump of clay for the body and added a head, breasts, and legs.

The Venus is one of hundreds of sculpted female figures from the prehistoric era that archaeologists have uncovered between Russia and northern Italy. These figures have symbolic qualities—they represent fertility and the source of life in a sculptural form. Those who possessed these elegantly modeled sculptures likely believed that the clay figures were imbued with the powers of the gods.

Baked Earth

By the time the ancient Egyptians built the Great Pyramid of Giza around 2560 BCE, symbolism and sculpture were inseparable. Religion dominated every aspect of Egyptian life, so each object was created as a work of symbolic art representing beliefs such as life after death and the godlike powers of the pharaohs.

The Egyptians used a type of clay ceramic known as terra-cotta (Italian for "baked earth") to make everything from lifelike human sculptures to dinnerware. Still used by sculptors today, terra-cotta is a mix of fine-grained dirt, water, and components such as sand and lime (calcium oxide). Terra-cotta has a distinctive brownish-orange color and has long been used to make bricks.

When artists use terra-cotta clay to create a sculpture, it is baked in a kiln, or oven, at a temperature of about 2,000°F (1,093°C). The earliest kilns were holes dug in the ground or carved into hillsides. The Egyptians had freestanding brick kilns fueled with wood, brush, and even animal dung. Modern kilns are gas- or electric-fired computer-controlled units. They can range in size from small studio units the size of a large garbage can to room-sized industrial ovens.

After it leaves the kiln, a terra-cotta sculpture can be finished with colored glaze, a glass-like substance made from various elements and minerals. Glaze was originally used by Egyptian and Chinese sculptors around 1,600 BCE. The ancient artists mixed compounds from sand, lime, and wood ash. The process of glazing clay sculptures has changed little since the time of the pharaohs. Glaze is applied to terra-cotta in a liquid form. The piece is then baked in a kiln for approximately eighteen hours. This process causes the glaze to vitrify, or transform, into a rock-hard permanence that can endure for millennia.

> **Words in Context**
> *glaze*
> Ceramic coatings made from silica sand, lead, or sodium, and colorings such as copper and magnesium.

Greek Figurines

Like the ancient Egyptians and Chinese, Greeks around the fifth century BCE also created terra-cotta sculptures. Baked in kilns that the Greeks referred to as *kaminos*, these small, mass-produced clay sculptures represented Greek deities, including Hermes, the messenger to the gods, and the fertility goddess Demeter. People

The Beehive Kiln

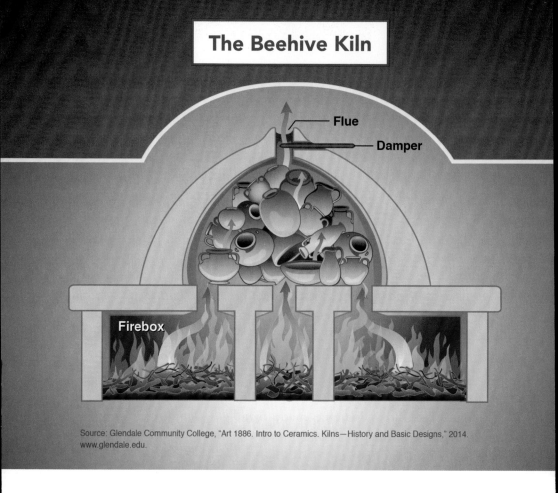

Source: Glendale Community College, "Art 1886. Intro to Ceramics. Kilns—History and Basic Designs," 2014. www.glendale.edu.

used the artistic figurines as religious offerings, leaving them at temple altars while petitioning the gods for luck, love, and revenge upon enemies. The prized terra-cotta sculptures were also buried with the dead.

Around the fourth century BCE, Greek artisans in the town of Tanagra mass-produced figurines that were appreciated for their variety of realistic poses and features. The sculptures possessed fine artistic details such as rippled folds in cloaks, flowing wraparound dresses, unusual wide-brimmed hats, and the coiffured hairstyles favored by style-conscious Greeks.

Tanagra figurines were around 12 inches (30 cm) high and created through the use of molds. Sculptors first shaped

Words in Context
vitrify
To change liquid glaze into a hard glassy substance through exposure to heat.

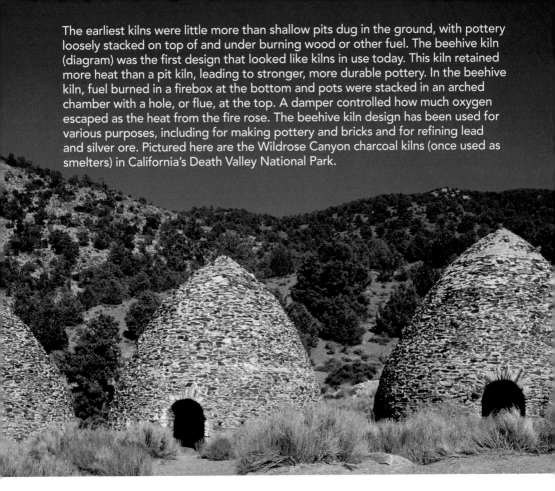

The earliest kilns were little more than shallow pits dug in the ground, with pottery loosely stacked on top of and under burning wood or other fuel. The beehive kiln (diagram) was the first design that looked like kilns in use today. This kiln retained more heat than a pit kiln, leading to stronger, more durable pottery. In the beehive kiln, fuel burned in a firebox at the bottom and pots were stacked in an arched chamber with a hole, or flue, at the top. A damper controlled how much oxygen escaped as the heat from the fire rose. The beehive kiln design has been used for various purposes, including for making pottery and bricks and for refining lead and silver ore. Pictured here are the Wildrose Canyon charcoal kilns (once used as smelters) in California's Death Valley National Park.

an original statue by hand and hardened it in a kiln. A thick layer of clay was pressed around the original to make a mold. This was then divided in half with a knife to create a hollow, two-sided mold that was also fired in the kiln. Once the mold was finished, artists pressed thin layers of soft clay into it by hand. As the clay dried, it contracted, or shrank, which made it easy to lift out of the mold.

The molding process was used to create numerous parts of a single sculpture. For example, one mold might be of a body; another of a head; and others of arms, legs, and other features. The more elaborate statues required up to fifteen molds. Graceful maidens were created carrying items such as fans, actors' masks, or mirrors, all produced in separate molds. The Greeks used a glue called *barbotine*, made from clay and water, to attach the various pieces of the sculpture to one another.

The final figurine was fired in a kiln at temperatures of about 1,110°F to 1,470°F (600 to 800°C). Tanagra figurines were finished not with expensive glaze, but with a coating called slip, made from a powdered clay and water mixture. This was fired at low temperatures. In the final step, Greek artisans decorated the statue with red, yellow, black, and pink paints made from natural mineral dyes.

> **Words in Context**
> *kiln*
> An oven used for baking clay items to harden them.

China's Terra-Cotta Army

Although the Tanagra figurines were elaborate, they could not compare to the work of Chinese sculptors in the third century BCE. The Chinese devised methods for producing life-sized terra-cotta sculptures of warriors in full battle regalia. And these sculptures were not made for the masses but for a single man—Emperor Qin Shi Huang, founder of China's first empire. The terra-cotta army was intended to guard an underground palace from which Qin would rule the universe after his death.

The army, created around 210 BCE, consists of approximately seven thousand glazed sculptures of soldiers ranging from about 5 feet 5 inches (1.7 m) to 6 feet (1.8 m) tall. Each figure originally held real weapons; the army's arsenal consisted of tens of thousands of metal-and-wood swords, axes, spears, lances, and crossbows. The warriors stood alongside hundreds of other terra-cotta sculptures, including 130 intricately detailed chariots, 670 horses, and numerous nonmilitary figures such as government officials, acrobats, and musicians.

The terra-cotta warriors appear fresh and alive, attesting to the skill of the artisans who created them. However, the people who created them worked under great pressure. Archaeologists have discovered letters written by the sculptors, and one artisan wrote to his mother, "I have to work carefully every day, if I paint the weapons incorrectly, my officer will punish me very severely."[2]

The massive sculpture site was discovered in March 1974 by farmers in Xi'an, China, who were digging a well in a field. The terra-cotta warriors were buried in four huge pits. The largest, 755 feet (230 m) long and 230 feet (70 m) wide, contains six thousand soldiers.

Glazes

Artists have used colored glazes to decorate clay sculptures for thousands of years. Glazes are mixed from three basic elements. The first is a glass-forming agent, most commonly silica, a common component of sand. When exposed to temperatures of 1,700°F (927°C) in a kiln during the glaze-firing process, the silica is vitrified, or melted onto the piece. Because this extreme temperature might also melt the clay, a second element of glaze, called the fluxing agent, is added. Fluxing agents, such as lead, boron, sodium, and potassium, help silica melt at lower temperatures. The third element of glaze, alumina, makes the other two ingredients more stable and viscous and thus prevents them from becoming too liquid and running off the piece.

Metal compounds add colors to glaze. Brightly colored glazes ranging from peacock green to bright reddish-brown are made from copper. Tin produces white. Iron, depending on its proportion in the mix, can create colors ranging from pale yellow to dark brown and black. Cobalt creates a blue glaze. Magnesium gives glaze a dull purple or a bright violet when mixed with cobalt.

Piecing Together the Warriors

Archaeologists believe the terra-cotta army was created over the course of thirty-seven years by a workforce that totaled more than 720,000. Workers first built the bodies and then added customized heads. The inner cores for the heads were made from solid lumps of clay. Additional clay was added to create about a dozen different head shapes. Sculptors then applied clay mouths, eyebrows, ears, noses, facial hair, and other features that gave each statue a unique appearance. Hairstyles fashioned from separate clay pieces were varied according to a warrior's job. Archers wore their hair in a rakish, tilted topknot with finely woven braids at the sides and back. Stable boys

Intricately detailed terra-cotta warriors guard the mausoleum of Chinese emperor Qin Shi Huang. Chinese artisans devised methods for producing life-sized terra-cotta sculptures of warriors in full battle regalia.

had their hair drawn into a simple bun at the back of the head. Light infantrymen were created wearing thick clay beards.

The bodies of the terra-cotta warriors were assembled in different sections from the feet up to the neck. At the bottom, large, square footplates held the heavy statues upright. Feet and legs of various shapes and sizes were built up from the footplates, formed complete with muscles and bones. Short pants representing the lower torso were placed on top of the legs.

The upper parts of the torso had to be hollow inside or the legs could not hold the weight of the clay. Each torso was made from bands of clay wound upward in a circular fashion. Layers were strengthened with thin strips of coarsely woven fabric called sackcloth. The torsos were finished with a variety of clothing, decorated according to rank. The backs of the coats worn by the generals appear to be decorated with many ribbons, all of which were carved in elaborate detail in the clay. Some generals are wearing protective armor—clay panels formed to look like lacquered leather.

When the torsos were finished they were dried in the shade. Sculptors then attached hollow arms. Hands and heads were attached, and the entire statue was fired in one of several huge kilns heated to about 1,830°F (1,000°C). After the terra-cotta was baked, glazes were applied and the works were heated again. Some of the warriors were elaborately painted with colorful glazes to appear lifelike; the long coats of the generals were decorated to imitate printed fabric, with a diamond pattern of green on a purple background. However, the colors faded over the centuries that the sculptures lay buried. The figures now appear steel gray.

When Qin died, work on his elaborate burial site ceased immediately. He was interred deep within the center of the tomb in a dirt mound. The most startlingly realistic terra-cotta sculptures ever made were entirely buried along with the emperor. Grass eventually grew over the site, and its contents were forgotten for centuries. Today, however, the terra-cotta army is considered unique among the world's collections of ancient sculptures.

A Terra-Cotta Saint

The terra-cotta warriors were created in a style known as realism, meaning the figures were made to look as realistic as possible. Realism was also central to the Italian Renaissance, a period of artistic rebirth lasting from about 1400 to 1600. During the Renaissance era, artists used clay to create lifelike statues of priests, saints, aristocrats, and kings. And clay reliefs—flat panels with raised sculptures on them—were used to illustrate scenes from the Bible as well as tales from ancient mythology, because few people at the time could read or afford books.

Words in Context
reliefs
Sculptures with raised or sunken figures carved into flat panels.

The Renaissance is mainly remembered for its marble and bronze sculptures. However, sculptor and architect Michelozzo di Bartolomeo created one of the most notable statues of the era from terra-cotta. The work, *St. John the Baptist*, was completed in 1452 and placed in the Basilica of the Most Holy Annunciation in Florence, Italy. The freestanding terra-cotta sculpture is more than 6 feet (1.8 m) high. St. John is depicted holding a cross and pointing to heaven with a solemn expression meant to inspire veneration and contemplation.

There is no mistaking Michelozzo's intent to create a work both artistic and reverent. But the sculptor had to overcome several technological problems. The Italians did not have kilns large enough to bake *St. John* when it was finished. This required Michelozzo to cut the raw clay sculpture into pieces. He separated the head and limbs from the body, cut the torso in two, and hollowed out sections so the feet and legs would not have to bear the weight of the clay.

After *St. John* was fired, Michelozzo reassembled it like a giant three-dimensional jigsaw puzzle. The various pieces were glued together with gesso, a mixture made of animal glue, chalk, pigment, and ground-up pottery. This was so expertly done that the piece appears seamless.

Gauguin's "Abnormal" Statues

In the nineteenth century the style of realism revered by Renaissance masters such as Michelozzo was rejected by Paul Gauguin, a Parisian painter and sculptor. Gauguin pioneered the modern art genre. Rather than create works of beauty that inspired reverence, modernists worked to express their personal emotions in their art, such as joy, despair, sorrow, and love.

Gauguin was fascinated with dramatic art created by the indigenous people who lived in the Caribbean, Central America, and Polynesia, the numerous islands scattered across the South Pacific. Although he was principally a painter, Gauguin began working with ceramics in the 1880s. In 1887 he created numerous ceramic sculptures inspired by Mexican and Polynesian deities. The sculptures defied acceptable artistic practices; they were misshapen, with irregular figures, and partially glazed with some parts deliberately left unfinished. The

One of the most notable terra-cotta statues of the Renaissance, *St. John the Baptist* (pictured), stands more than six feet high. Sculptor Michelozzo di Bartolomeo overcame several technological problems to create a work that is both artistic and reverent.

surfaces contained uneven textures, bubbles, smears, and even fingerprints. Although Gauguin was captivated by the sculptures, he playfully called them monstrosities in a letter to his friend, painter Félix Bracquemond: "If you are curious to see all the small products of my extreme madness coming out of a kiln—55 pieces in good condition—you will scream loudly in the presence of my monstrosities but I am convinced that these things will fascinate you."[3]

When Gauguin displayed his ceramic sculptures, they were mocked by critics who labeled them primitive and savage. As critic

Félix Fénéon wrote in 1888, "What dishonored, inauspicious and harsh stoneware, he [Gauguin] gave life to: haggard faces with widely spaced large eyes, or with small eyes set adjacent to the snub-nose . . . works of an abnormal and deformed geometry."[4]

Disgusted by such attitudes, Gauguin moved to Polynesia in the 1890s, where he created dozens of paintings of Tahitian women. In 1894 Gauguin's Polynesian inspirations led him to create *Oviri*, his most famous sculpture. Oviri is a Tahitian deity of death and mourning whose name translates as "savage" or "wild." Although *Oviri* is only 30 inches (76 cm) high, Gauguin depicted the goddess as chillingly ferocious. She is crushing the life out of a bloody wolf cub while its mother lies dead at her feet. This scene was symbolic of Oviri's power over life as well as her indifference to death.

Troubled by ill health, drug addiction, legal problems, and poverty, Gauguin called *Oviri* "his murderess"[5] and viewed the work as an expression of his profound depression. However, painter and art critic Albert Aurier was dazzled by *Oviri* and Gauguin's other clay figures, writing: "How to describe these strange, barbaric, savage ceramics in which, sublime potter, he has kneaded more soul than clay?"[6]

Picasso and the Spirits

Gauguin died in 1903 at age fifty-four, but his work inspired the Spanish painter and sculptor Pablo Picasso, whose fame was rising rapidly in the early 1900s. According to art critic John Blee, "It was Gauguin's appreciation of Tahitian art, whose influence he incorporated into his own work, which led directly to Picasso's appreciation of African art."[7]

In 1907 Picasso was twenty-six years old and living in Paris. His interest in African art led him to visit the Ethnological Museum located in the Trocadéro Palace near the Eiffel Tower. The museum was filled with carved African masks and clay statues called fetishes, said to have supernatural powers. Picasso was attracted to these ancient religious icons that had been created by African shamans, or spiritual leaders. Shamans used the fetishes as a way to communicate with mystical spirits to attract luck, heal the sick, and ward off evil.

Magical African Sculptures

When Pablo Picasso visited Paris's Ethnological Museum in 1907, he was both repelled and attracted by the magical significance of the carved African masks and statues. Picasso later told French minister of culture André Malraux:

> I was all alone. I wanted to get away. But I didn't leave. I stayed. I stayed. I understood that it was very important: something was happening to me, right? The masks weren't just like any other pieces of sculpture. Not at all. They were magic things. . . . They were against everything—against unknown, threatening spirits. . . . I understood; I too am against everything. I too believe that everything is unknown, that everything is an enemy! Everything! Not the details—women, children, babies, tobacco, playing—but the whole of it! I understood what the [Africans] used their sculpture for. . . . They were weapons. To help people avoid coming under the influence of spirits again, to help them become independent. They're tools. If we give spirits a form, we become independent. I understood why I was a painter.

Quoted in André Malraux, *Picasso's Mask*. New York: Holt, Rinehart and Winston, 1976, pp. 10–11.

Picasso went back to his studio and began making sketches featuring the angular heads, geometric features, and distorted body shapes found in the African sculptures. These African influences led Picasso to paint one of his most famous works, the 1907 painting *Les*

Demoiselles d'Avignon. Today the painting is seen as one of the first made in the cubist style conceived by Picasso. The five women in the painting barely resemble rounded human figures. Their bodies are cube-like, with blocky, angular torsos and sharp, distorted facial features. Two of the figures are wearing what appear to be abstractly painted African masks.

Words in Context
cubist
Describes a style of painting or sculpting in which there is little detail and objects are represented by chunky blocks, geometric shapes, and cylinders.

It was not until Picasso settled in the town of Vallauris in southern France in 1947 that he took a great interest in clay sculpture. The region is known for its mineral-rich soil, which has been used to make pottery for two millennia.

Picasso had two young children when he moved to Vallauris, and the ceramics he created there reflect a happiness rarely seen in his work. The sculptures are decorated with witty, charming designs featuring bulls, birds, and curvaceous female figures. Picasso called these ceramics "sculpture without tears"[8] because the fired clay objects were small and easy to handle. Between 1947 and 1962 he produced about three thousand pieces of clay and ceramic sculpture. Picasso went on to become one of history's best-known artists, a pioneer whose work defined twentieth-century art.

By creating sculptures based on indigenous art, Picasso and Gauguin brought terra-cotta full circle from its ancient roots. As a link to the gods, as a way to express reverence and emotion, and as a substance to create a standing army, clay has served a noble purpose in the artistic development of humankind for more than 350 centuries.

Chapter Two

Inspiration in Stone

Ancient Greek sculptors produced some of the world's most celebrated works of art, and the marble sculpture *Laocoön and His Sons* represents classical Greek art in its most passionate and dramatic form. In Greek mythology Laocoön was a high priest who was killed, along with his sons, by two serpents. The violent death scene was immortalized in marble around 200 BCE by three sculptors from the Greek island of Rhodes: Agesander, Athenodoros, and Polydorus.

Laocoön's stark agony is carved into every one of his features: his wrinkled forehead, squinted eyes, and half-open mouth. His sons convey a childlike innocence even as the serpents entwine them in a deadly embrace. After German art historian J.J. Winckelmann viewed *Laocoön and His Sons* at the Vatican in Rome in 1755, he wrote: "The pain is revealed in all the muscles and sinews of his body, and we ourselves can almost feel it. . . . This pain, however, expresses itself with no sign of rage in his face or in his entire bearing. . . . The physical pain and the nobility of soul are distributed with equal strength over the entire body and are held in balance with one another."[9]

The fact that a silent piece of stone could move Winckelmann to "almost feel" Laocoön's anguish is a testament to the art of carved sculpture. Talented sculptors can shape stone into forms that express dramatic stories, convey beauty, or move viewers to laughter or tears. Because of this characteristic, subtractive, or carved, sculptures are some of the most famous works of art in the world.

A Statue Inside a Stone

A subtractive sculptor uses a chisel, mallet, and other tools to subtract material from a piece of stone. As Michelangelo described sculpting, "every block of stone has a statue inside it and it is the task of the sculptor to discover it."[10]

Subtractive sculptures may be created from many different stones, including granite, marble, limestone, sandstone, onyx, and alabaster. Because of stone's extreme hardness, working with it requires great patience and skill. Despite the difficulties, however, sculptors have been carving rock for countless millennia. Some of the oldest subtractive sculptures were created by the ancient Egyptians around five thousand years ago. Although they had a very limited range of tools, the Egyptians were able to create gigantic and magnificent sculptures that have survived into the twenty-first century.

The Great Sphinx

One of the most famous—and largest—sculptures in the world stands in front of the Great Pyramid of Giza in Egypt. The work, the Great Sphinx of Giza, was carved from limestone cliffs around 2900 BCE. With the body of a lion and the head of a pharaoh, the Sphinx is 20 feet (6 m) wide and more than 66 feet (20 m) high, making it the largest monolith, or stand-alone statue, in the world.

Since its creation around 2550 BCE, the Sphinx has evoked a sense of mystery and wonder. The huge statue fuses the images of a lion and a pharaoh into a single powerful creature. But although the Sphinx is a colossal achievement, it was more than mere art to the Egyptians. Lions embody strength and ferocity and were seen as guardians against evil. Combined with the head of a pharaoh, the Sphinx represents royal power at its greatest strength.

The Golden Age of Greece

The Sphinx was created by workers using stone hammers and copper chisels to carve the sculpture into the rock cliffs. The Egyptians also used copper saws and wood-handled drills with copper or stone drill bits. Because copper is a soft metal that dulls quickly and needs to be resharpened after only a few blows, it is estimated that it took about one hundred artisans three years to complete the massive sculpture.

By the time of what is known as the golden age of classical Greek art, from 480 to 323 BCE, sculptors were carving white limestone and marble using much more sophisticated tools made of iron. A hammer-like tool with a sharp head, called a pick, was used to chip away the surface of the stone and shape it in a rough manner. Toothed chisels with numerous sharp teeth were used for coarse carving after the initial work was finished. Flat chisels with sharp edges of varying widths were used to refine the work of toothed chisels. Small hand drills were used to sculpt fine details. Finally, the surface of the stone was smoothed with an abrasive powder called emery, a finely ground granular rock used today to make fingernail files called emery boards.

All manner of hammers and chisels are used by sculptors who work with marble and stone. Here, a sculptor demonstrates the use of a round, steel carving hammer and carving chisel.

Many larger Greek sculptures were not carved from a single block of stone but from several pieces; for example, the three nearly life-sized figures in *Laocoön and His Sons*, along with the huge serpents, were carved from seven separate interlocking pieces of marble. The pieces were joined with thin metal rods called dowels that were inserted into holes drilled in each piece. After the pieces were joined, they were bonded with molten lead or cement made from powdered marble. This technique was also used to join finished sculptures to base plates.

A Sculpture Renaissance

Classical Greek culture was absorbed by the Romans around 320 BCE. The Romans adapted many techniques perfected by the sculptors of Greece. However, Roman artists lacked the artistic skills of the Greeks, according to art historian Hans Koepf: "From the Greeks the Romans took over materials and chiseling techniques of the utmost perfection, but hardly the creative talents. At the outset, Rome imported Grecian works and later commissioned Greek artists to copy famous masterpieces."[11]

It was not until the fifteenth century that the creativity of the Greeks was matched—in fact, surpassed—by Italian sculptors. During the Renaissance, sculptors produced their works in essentially the same manner as the Greeks, with hammers, drills, and a variety of chisels. The Italians were inspired by classical Greek composition, or arrangement of figures. But Renaissance artists perfected a style of physical realism even beyond the scope of the Greeks.

> **Words in Context**
>
> *composition*
> The organization of visual elements in a work of art.

The Renaissance rebirth of sculpture was led by Michelangelo, born in 1475. Michelangelo exhibited an incredible talent for sculpting when he was an apprentice in Florence. When he was only sixteen, Michelangelo created the complex marble relief *Battle of the Centaurs*. The relief is based on a Greek myth that depicts a fight between the Lapith tribe and the half-human, half-horse centaurs. Into a piece of flat marble only about 1 yard square (84 cm by 90 cm), Michelangelo carved several dozen figures, many of them writhing in violent battle, their bodies twisted in anguish.

Michelangelo's *Pietà*

The word *pietà* is used to define any statue of the Virgin Mary grieving over the body of Jesus. However, the *Pietà* created by Michelangelo around 1498 demonstrates why the sculptor was nicknamed "the Divine One." In 1550 Italian painter and art historian Giorgio Vasari described the heavenly features Michelangelo was able to carve into stone:

> Among the lovely things to be seen in the work, to say nothing of the divinely beautiful draperies, is the body of Christ; nor let anyone think to see greater beauty . . . or more mastery of art in any body, or a nude with more detail in the muscles, veins, and nerves over the framework of the bones, nor yet a corpse more similar than this to a real corpse. Here is perfect sweetness in the expression of the head, harmony in the joints and attachments of the arms, legs, and trunk, and the pulses and veins so wrought, that in truth Wonder herself must marvel that the hand of a craftsman should have been able to execute so divinely and so perfectly, in so short a time, a work so admirable; and it is certainly a miracle that a stone without any shape at the beginning should ever have been reduced to such perfection as Nature is scarcely able to create in the flesh.

Giorgio Vasari, trans. Gaston du C. De Vere, *Lives of the Most Eminent Painters Sculptors, and Architects.* London: Medici Society, 1915, p. 14.

In 1498 Michelangelo created the *Pietà*, a sculpture portraying the Virgin Mary holding the body of Jesus. The work, displayed at St. Peter's Basilica in Vatican City, brought its creator widespread recognition. This led to the commission of his most famous sculpture. In 1500 Michelangelo was contracted by the Florence Guild of Wool

Merchants to create a massive statue of the figure of David, who slays the giant Goliath in a story from the Bible. The guild presented Michelangelo with a giant chunk of marble weighing an estimated 12,000 pounds (5,443 kg) and standing 18 feet (5.5 m) tall. The stone was originally cut from the famous quarries of Carrara, Italy, in 1466, after which the sculptor Agostino di Duccio attempted to carve it into a statue of David.

Work on *David* stopped for reasons unknown after Agostino marked out the shape of the legs, feet, and drapery. The marble sat outdoors in the courtyard of Florence Cathedral, neglected for more than three decades; the wool merchants noted in a contract with Michelangelo that the narrow block of stone was "badly roughed out."[12] However, the Carrara marble was so valuable that wool merchants insisted that it be used.

Carving the Giant

The twenty-six-year-old Michelangelo referred to the coarse marble as the Giant. In September 1501 he began chipping away at the stone to create the slim, muscular figure of David. For the next twenty-eight months he worked in secrecy. Michelangelo understood that another sculptor had tried and failed to bring the marble to life; should he fail similarly, he did not want this fact to be widely known. On the other hand, he also knew that success would enhance his reputation as a master sculptor.

Words in Context
musculature
The system or arrangement of muscles in a body or part of a body.

Michelangelo worked from a wooden scaffold built around the marble, pounding away with hammers and chisels. After the fifty-year-old artist Leonardo da Vinci saw his young rival at work, he noted Michelangelo "looks like a baker. The marble dust flours all over him and his back is covered in a snowstorm of chips."[13]

In 1504 Michelangelo finally unveiled *David* to the public. It was instantly recognized as a remarkable depiction of flawless musculature, flesh, and bone. David's pose, attitude, and facial features were works of eternal perfection. According to art historian Sheldon

A worker cuts a large chunk of marble at the famous quarry in Carrara, Italy. Michelangelo's *David* was carved from a 12,000-pound block of Carrara marble.

Cheney, the statue also revealed Michelangelo's heightened reverence of the marble itself. Cheney says that Michelangelo exhibited "a passionate devotion to the inner central elements that constitute sculptural art, devotion to the integrity of the stone block, to the living qualities of massiveness and majesty and power. . . . Michelangelo is a sculptor apart, mystical, contemplative, in love with the stone."[14]

Michelangelo considered himself a sculptor, not a painter. However, four years after finishing *David*, he was commissioned by Pope Julius II to paint the ceiling of the Vatican's Sistine Chapel, 68 feet (20.7 m) above the floor. Like *David*, the ceiling of the Sistine Chapel, completed in 1512, is one of the world's most enduring masterpieces.

Creating a Natural Appearance

David influenced generations of artists, including Auguste Rodin, a sculptor widely acclaimed as the father of modern sculpture. Rodin, born in Paris in 1840, visited Florence when he was thirty-six and was dazzled by *David*. He filled his notebooks with sketches of Michelangelo's numerous sculptures and set out to create nineteenth-century versions of the Renaissance master's work. Art critic Grace Glueck explains:

> Rodin had an ambitious interest in Michelangelo. Aside from marveling at his technical prowess in conveying the torques and tensions of the figure, Rodin was gripped by Michelangelo's spiritual intensity, and he believed that his expressive art stood for the essence of the Italian people. In his own work and persona, Rodin aspired to represent the national genius of France.[15]

At the time, the artistic brilliance of France was exemplified by artists like Claude Monet and Pierre-Auguste Renoir, who pioneered a painting technique called impressionism. Rather than use the somber hues of Renaissance painters, the impressionists used bright colors. And while Renaissance painters worked inside studios, the impressionists painted outdoors to capture fleeting moments of sunlight and shadows on their subjects.

Like other impressionists, Rodin wanted his works to appear spontaneous. To accomplish this he had his models wander freely around his studio. This diverged from traditional sculptors who posed models in stiff, still positions and created awkward, artificial-looking sculptures.

With his unusual technique, Rodin produced sculptures that are remarkable for their warm, natural appearance. To further heighten the unstructured feel, Rodin carved tiny bumps and hollows into the stone. These small variations reflected impressionistic patterns of light and shadow. As a result, the surfaces of the stone figures in Rodin's sculptures such as *Vase des Titans* (1878) and *The Kiss* (1889) appear soft, silky, and almost flesh-like.

Impressionism in the United States

While Rodin personally sculpted many of his works, he was also an astute businessman. His work was in great demand, and to profit from this he set up a large workshop in Paris and filled it with highly trained artisans and assistants.

Rodin's workshop attracted aspiring sculptors from around the globe who wished to learn from the master. Among them was Gutzon Borglum, a sculptor born in Idaho in 1867, who was greatly influenced by Rodin's impressionistic light-catching sculpting techniques.

Back in the United States in 1912, Borglum carved a dramatic, 6-ton (5.4 metric ton) marble bust of Abraham Lincoln for display in the White House (the sculpture is now on display at the US Capitol building). Borglum created *Lincoln* with deep whorls and hollows in the face. This impressionist technique gives a sense of sadness and suffering to the president who presided over the bloody Civil War. The deep-set eyes and protruding lips give Lincoln the look of a weary saint.

Carving America's Achievements

Although he was influenced by French art, Borglum was a passionate patriot who founded a new style he called American art. Borglum believed that art in the United States should be created by Americans to memorialize American accomplishments. He was offended that buildings, parks, and courtyards in the United States were decorated with sculptures made by European artists. Around 1915 Borglum wrote that American art should be "built into, cut into, the crust of this earth so that those records would have to melt, or by wind be worn to dust before the record . . . [could] perish from this earth."[16]

Gutzon Borglum rides an aerial tram in 1935 to check on the carving of Thomas Jefferson's face during construction of his colossal Mount Rushmore sculpture. The faces of four US presidents were carved into a granite cliff in South Dakota's Black Hills.

Borglum believed that four presidents—George Washington, Thomas Jefferson, Theodore Roosevelt, and Abraham Lincoln—were the greatest Americans in history. In 1927 Borglum and a team of four hundred workers began carving sculptures of these historical figures' heads into the 450-foot-high (137 m) granite cliffs of Mount Rushmore in South Dakota.

No sculpture the size of Mount Rushmore had ever been attempted. The heads of the presidents seem to emerge from the rock on a scale previously unimaginable. Each is more than 60 feet (18 m) high, as tall

Carving Mount Rushmore

When Gutzon Borglum decided to carve the faces of four presidents into Mount Rushmore in South Dakota, no artist had ever attempted to create a scupture on such a grand scale. Instead of hiring sculptors, Borglum employed miners who were experienced in moving large amounts of rock. The *American Experience* website provides details about the sculpting of Mount Rushmore:

> The workers were expected to be at the top of the mountain by 7 a.m. in the summer, or 7:30 in fall and winter. Once up top, men would be fitted into leather harnesses designed by Borglum himself, and lowered down the face of the mountain by means of cables attached to hand-cranked winches.... [Dynamite] was used to blast the rock into a general shape. To control the blasting, sticks of dynamite would be cut down to make smaller charges, up to 70 for one detonation.
>
> The drillers then removed stone to within six inches of the finished surfaces. The drillers carried Chicago-Pneumatic jackhammers, weighing over 75 pounds, with a hose for the compressed air powering the drill. These were not the easiest tools to handle—especially when hanging in a harness on the side of a mountain....
>
> Then the carvers would take over. By drilling a series of shallow holes in a closely-spaced grid, and then removing these grids by drilling obliquely—a process they called "honeycombing"—the carvers got very close to finished surface. The carvers did the final finishing using smaller handheld pneumatic hammers.

American Experience, "Carving the Mountain," PBS, 2013. www.pbs.org.

as a six-story building. The entire memorial covers 1,278 acres (517 ha). Washington's nose is 21 feet (6.4 m) long, and his mouth is 18 feet (5.5 m) wide. The mole on Lincoln's cheek is about the size of a basketball hoop.

Before beginning the work, Borglum drew upon his impressionist training. He spent days watching the sun and clouds and the changing light on the cliffs. Viewers today can appreciate Borglum's efforts as the changing light and shadows appear to make the faces on the mountain move slightly as the moments pass. The movements are particularly obvious in the 11-foot-wide (3.4 m) eyes of the presidents. Workers carefully hollowed out deep pupils to give them a living appearance in the changing light. The eyes also seem to reveal the thoughts and passions of each president. Washington and Lincoln stare wisely into infinity, while Jefferson's eyes are turned toward the skies, as if envisioning a promising future. The penetrating gaze of Roosevelt, the most recent president on the mountain, seems to look down on the tourists below.

Borglum designed and built the massive sculpture to last for the ages. As he stated in a speech when the face of Jefferson was unveiled in 1936:

> I am allowing an extra three inches on all the features of the various Presidents in order to provide stone for the wear and tear of the elements, which cuts the granite down one inch every hundred thousand years. Three inches would require three-hundred thousand years to bring the work down to the point that I would like to finish it. In other words, the work will not be done for another three hundred thousand years, as it should be.[17]

Mount Rushmore was finally completed in 1941, fourteen years after the carving began. In all, the workers removed 500,000 tons (453,592 metric tons) of granite, blasting and carving as much as 120 feet (36.6 m) into the original cliffs. Mount Rushmore hosts nearly 2 million visitors each year and remains one of the most astounding sculptures of all time. Although it might lack the sinew and emotions of *Laocoön and His Sons* or *David*, Borglum's masterpiece follows a long tradition. Whether a sculptor is using a chisel or a jackhammer, some of the world's most memorable sculptures have been created to honor heroes in stone.

Chapter Three

Beauty in Bronze

Sculpting in clay, stone, or bone can be a solitary activity, performed by an individual artist with a singular vision. This is not the case for sculpting with bronze and other metals. Casting requires a team of artisans who work together in an industrial setting to make molds, pour red-hot metal, and apply finishes to the cast sculpture. Sculptors of bronze must combine artistic sensitivities with the technological skills of a foundry worker and the strength of a laborer.

Though historians are unsure exactly when bronze casting was invented, artisans were engaging in the process in China, India, and the Middle East around five thousand years ago. Around the sixth century BCE, Greek artists were casting bronze to create statuary for public places. These sculptures depicted musicians, artists, soldiers on chariots, victorious athletes, battling animals, gods, and mythological scenes.

> **Words in Context**
> *statuary*
> Numerous statues or the art of creating numerous statues.

Bronze statues could last for centuries. In the first century CE, the Romans placed a three-hundred-year-old bronze of a mastiff hound in front of the revered temple of Juno, the queen of the gods. The stewards who guarded the ancient Greek bronze had to lay their lives on the line to protect the sculpture. Around 78 CE, Roman historian Pliny the Elder noted:

Art has made extraordinary progress, in technique first and afterward in audacity. As an example of successful technique I shall mention a figure representing neither god nor man . . . in the temple of Juno, a bronze dog licking his wound. The wonderful workmanship and absolutely lifelike treatment are sufficiently proved not only by the sacred spot where the work was dedicated, but also by the unusual guarantee demanded for it. . . . It was a public ordinance that the curators should pledge their lives for its safety.[18]

Creating a lifelike bronze dog worth dying for required specially skilled and highly organized artists. Those who engaged in the early industrial practice of bronze casting worked with valuable raw metals extracted from mines; bronze is an alloy of copper and tin, sometimes mixed with small amounts of lead and silver. Artists were trained to mix the metals into combinations that produced various sheens and colors. This required them to understand how the metals react chemically when exposed to high heat. And sculptors were charged with transforming the raw materials into high-quality artworks worthy of honoring gods and heroes. Little wonder, then, that those who worked in bronze were widely revered. As bronze sculptor Christian Hauser explains, "The 'metal man' was elevated to the rank of demigod or held in awe as a being endowed with divine or magic powers. Only such powers could explain the ability to modify a part of the world by fire . . . creating something new out of what could be found in nature."[19]

> **Words in Context**
> *alloy*
> A mixture of metals; bronze is an alloy of copper and tin, with silver and lead sometimes added to change the color.

Donatello's *David*

The bronze traditions established by the Greeks remained in use for centuries. By the Renaissance era bronze was seen as a prime vehicle for artistic exploration. Among the dozens of famed sculptors of the time, Donatello was a pioneer in bronze.

Born in Florence in 1386, Donatello was a master of realism and composition. He combined these skills with the complex bronze casting methods of classical Greece. As art historian Giorgio Vasari wrote in 1550: "Donatello was so admirable in knowledge, in judgment, and in the practice of his art that he may be said to have been the first to illustrate the art of sculpture among the moderns."[20]

Donatello instilled his sculptures with dramatic emotions and personality. His bronze statue *David*, created around 1436, is remarkable for the posture and animated features that give the sculpture lifelike qualities. *David*'s body is softly rounded, almost feminine, and he is wearing a mysterious smile. The figure stands with a sword, and the severed head of the giant Goliath rests on his foot, suggesting that the battle with the giant has just ended. According to art historian Bruce Cole, "By so energizing the figure, Donatello has made a statue different from any of its . . . predecessors; it is no longer just the image but the personality and presence of David."[21]

Judith's Cold Defiance

David was a little over 5 feet (1.5 m) high and was the first freestanding bronze statue created since the classical Greek era. *David* was unsupported because it was intended to be set against a wall and viewed only from the front. This was not the case, however, with Donatello's grand

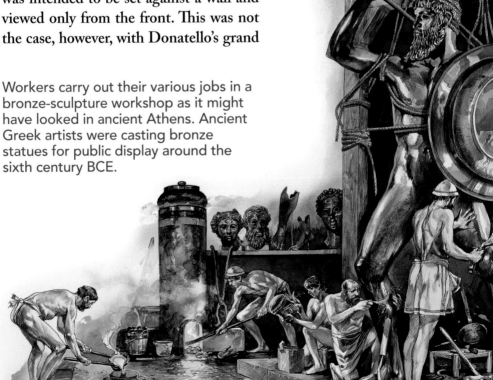

Workers carry out their various jobs in a bronze-sculpture workshop as it might have looked in ancient Athens. Ancient Greek artists were casting bronze statues for public display around the sixth century BCE.

work *Judith and Holofernes*, which is meant to be viewed in the round, or from all angles. Donatello based the bronze on another biblical story in which a hero beheads an adversary; in this case the sculpture portrays Judith slaying the invading general Holofernes, whom she kills to save the besieged city of Bethulia.

Judith and Holofernes, created between 1455 and 1460, is massive, nearly 8 feet (2.4 m) tall. The work exhibits the strength, bravery, and power of Judith, whose sword remains raised as if she is about to strike again. Her face exhibits a cold defiance as her vanquished foe slumps at her feet. Donatello's depiction of Holofernes is admired for its realistic depiction of the dead; the figure's mouth is agape, and its arm dangles uselessly at an odd angle.

Lost Wax Casting

No records exist that describe Donatello's exact casting techniques. However, according to twentieth-century research by art historians, *Judith and Holofernes* was made from eleven separate pieces using an ancient technique called lost wax casting. With this method, molten bronze is poured into a mold that has been created from a wax model. The complex technique, first used around 3500 BCE in India, allows skilled sculptors to create extremely detailed bronze sculptures.

The first step in the lost wax casting process requires the sculptor to make a complete, detailed sculpture from clay. After the sculpture is finished, the artist works with a mold maker, who creates a clay or plaster mold of the sculpture. When the mold is complete, the original sculpture is removed from it. Liquefied wax, heated to 210°F (99°C), is then poured into the mold and allowed to harden. This produces an exact duplicate of the original sculpture in wax. The wax mold is then finished; the sculptor uses knives, sanders, and heated irons to remove imperfections, such as the seam formed where the two halves of the model were joined. The detailing process is called wax chasing.

A new mold is then made around the wax sculpture, with holes called gates that will later allow the sculptor to pour in liquefied bronze. The mold is baked in a slowly heated kiln at a low heat of about 250°F (121°C). The name of the process, lost wax casting, originates from this step: The model is "lost" when the wax melts and flows out of the mold. The mold is left in the kiln and the tem-

The "Dance of the Pour"

Lost wax casting is a complex process that has changed little over the centuries. Sculptors Piero Mussi and Mavis McClure call the step of casting molten bronze into a mold the "Dance of the Pour." At least three artisans called casters are required to perform this dangerous task.

The Dance of the Pour begins at the crucible furnace, built from concrete and specially hardened fire brick. The center of the furnace holds a heavy graphite or porcelain cup, called a crucible. Bronze bars called ingots are liquefied at 2,100°F (1,149°C). The crucible is then lifted from the furnace by two artisans called lead casters, who use either long tongs with extended handles or a crane. Another caster, wearing fireproof mitts, protective clothing, and goggles, guides and balances the crucible as it moves over the mold. This caster is called the dead man because the job is very hazardous; the crucible can weigh more than 400 pounds (181 kg), and casters engaged in this act are exposed to toxic fumes and the possibility of extreme burns while handling the molten metal. Once the crucible is in place, the bronze is poured quickly into the mold and allowed to cool for about one hour. The bronze sculpture can then be removed and finished.

Quoted in Piero Mussi and Mavis McClure, "Bronze Sculpture: The Art of Lost Wax," ModernSculpture.com, 2000. www.modernsculpture.com.

perature is slowly raised to 1,100°F (593°C). The mold bakes at this temperature for twelve to thirty-six hours and becomes sufficiently hardened to receive the molten bronze without cracking.

Final Steps

While the mold is baking, copper and tin are heated in a furnace until they liquefy. The molten bronze is poured into the finished mold, which is moved to a sand pit to cool. When it has cooled sufficiently to be handled, the mold is chipped off, or divested, with a hammer and chisel. Any material remaining on the sculpture is removed. The final sculpture is chased, or finished smooth. Finally, a finisher hand polishes the piece and covers it with a patina, a colored coating produced by treatment with various chemicals. Three compounds form the basis for most patinas: ferric nitrate produces reds and browns, cupric nitrate creates greens and blues, and sulphurated potash produces black.

Lost wax casting is complicated, dangerous, and time-consuming, but it can be used to produce finely detailed sculptures. From the 1600s through the 1800s, European sculptors used the process to produce highly decorative and functional bronze objects such as candelabras and clocks.

> **Words in Context**
> *patina*
> A desirable tarnish that forms on copper and bronze as a result of mild, chemically induced corrosion.

The Thinker

In the mid-nineteenth century, European sculptors began using a process called sand casting, which was much less complex than lost wax casting. Sand casting was used to produce hollow sculptures. The process began when a sculptor made a model from wood, clay, or plaster. A second, slightly smaller duplicate was made of the original model. The first model was pressed into a special type of moist sand, creating an imprint of the original. The slightly smaller model was set into the mold and secured with pins to keep it away from the imprint in the sand. Molten bronze was poured into the narrow space between the sand and the smaller mold. Large sculptures made with sand casting were sometimes strengthened with an inner framework called an armature. Unlike lost wax casting, sand-cast molds could be used repeatedly to make numerous sculptures.

Successful sculptors created sand-cast bronzes primarily for two purposes. Large statues were produced in art studios for wealthy clients; smaller, decorative bronzes were mass-produced for average citizens. Art curator Patrick Elliott explains why the small bronzes were so popular: "Bronze had two distinct advantages over marble; first it was possible to make small sculptures crammed with narrative

Lost Wax Casting

Artists who create bronze sculptures often use a technique known as lost wax casting. In this process the artist begins with a clay sculpture of the piece he or she wishes to create **(1)**. A rubber mold with a shell, sometimes called a mother mold, is made **(2)**. Hot wax is poured into the mold **(3)**, creating a hollow wax cast **(4)**. Wax rods or wires called sprues are then attached to the model **(5)**. The model and sprues are encased in a type of plaster of paris called investment **(6)**. The sprues are left to stick out of the investment; they will later become the passageways through which bronze enters the mold. The wax inside the mold is burned and melted away **(7)**. Heated, liquified bronze is poured into the cavity that is left behind **(8)**. Once the bronze cools, the plaster cast is broken to reveal the sculpture **(9)**.

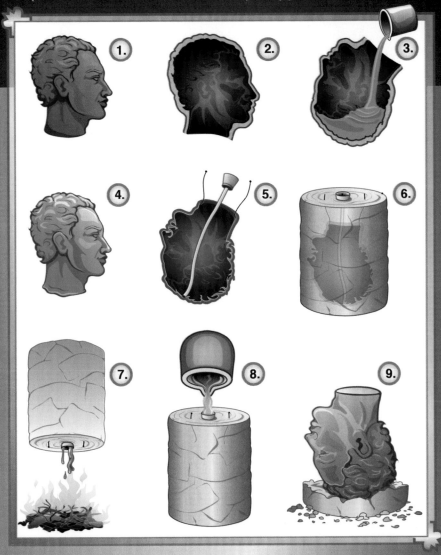

detail—the kind of detail you simply could not get with a chisel in a small-scale carving. And secondly, once a sculptor had made a model, it could be cast in countless copies, much like a book or [art] print."[22]

By the 1870s bronze was big business in Paris, where six hundred different companies employed seventy-five hundred workers involved in model making, sand casting, and finishing. Auguste Rodin was among the most famous artists who took advantage of this trend. Between 1898 and 1918 Rodin's marble masterpiece *The Kiss* was reproduced in three hundred different bronze versions of various sizes. And even as replicas of his works were displayed in living rooms and parlors throughout the world, Rodin remained an artistic innovator and influential trailblazer in the world of large bronze statuary.

The impressionist Rodin created bronze figures with small surface gouges, bumps, and hollows. This gave the human figures lifelike skin that reflected shadows and light. Rodin was also the first sculptor to leave his large bronzes unfinished in the back or on the sides. Rodin wanted the public to better understand how the sculptures were made. Rather than hide the armature, Rodin allowed viewers to peer into the work and see how the piece was constructed. According to Elliott, this practice "served to highlight the creative process involved in the making of a bronze sculpture, declaring in effect that artistic representation was . . . one of invention and freedom."[23]

The culmination of Rodin's creativity may be seen in his most famous work, *The Thinker*. The bronze *Thinker* portrays a life-sized nude male sitting on a rock deep in thought, with his chin resting on his hand. Rodin created the first version of the statue, which was about 28 inches (71 cm) tall, for the entryway of a proposed art museum in Paris, which was never built. In 1904 Rodin created an enlarged version of *The Thinker*, which was 73 inches (185 cm) high.

With its pose and composition, *The Thinker* represents common aspects of human nature. The figure's arched back, furrowed brow, and hand curled at the wrist are universal symbols of an emotional person lost in deep contemplation. As the Musée Rodin website

Promoting Large-Scale Public Art

In the twenty-first century giant outdoor metal sculptures are widely featured in parks, public gardens, and art museums. This was rarely the case in 1966, however, when the Lippincott Foundry was established to produce large-scale metal sculptures in an artist-friendly environment. The Lippincott website provides a brief history of this era:

> With 25-foot ceilings, overhead cranes, state-of-the-art lighting and giant bay doors, [the Lippincott Foundry] was indeed the ideal manufacturing space: an artist's studio writ large. . . . [The] fifteen-acre field surrounding the Lippincott factory became an informal sculpture park visited by area residents, student groups, and art professionals from around the world. The importance of showing the work in this fashion should not be overlooked. In the early days of the company, large-scale modern sculpture was not much in evidence. There was little new public art in cities, and most museums and galleries did not have adequate space to show larger sculptures. The pieces on display at Lippincott offered prospective collectors, both private and public, a chance to see works realized at large scale and to develop a greater understanding of the impact and importance of this work. With a crew size of between 12 and 24 workers over the years, Lippincott remained a relevant and active sculpture fabricating establishment right up to 1994 when the lease on the building ended.

Jonathan Lippincott, "History," Lippincott, 2013. www.lippincottsculpture.com.

explains, *The Thinker* is "both a being with a tortured body, almost a damned soul, and a free-thinking man, determined to transcend his suffering through poetry . . . [the] image of a man lost in thought, but whose powerful body suggests a great capacity for action."[24]

Rodin created twenty-eight identical castings of *The Thinker*, which today are on display in Japan, Europe, and North America. The statue was also replicated in various sizes in marble, clay, plaster, and bronze after Rodin's death. It remains one of the most recognizable sculptures in the world.

The *Broken Obelisk*

Rodin worked with numerous Paris foundries to produce his bronze sculptures. However, there were few comparable facilities for American artists in the United States. Most American foundries were engaged in industrial production, using established methods to mass-produce specific products such as cars, steel girders, and appliances. Large foundries were generally unwilling to work with artists who wished to forge one-of-a-kind sculptures.

This situation did not change until well past the mid-twentieth century. By the 1960s a growing number of artists were designing outdoor sculptures for display at parks, campuses, and urban settings. These sculptors were limited to creating relatively small works in their studios until 1966, when a unique facility opened in North Haven, Connecticut. The Lippincott Foundry, established by Donald Lippincott and Roxanne Everett, was a place where sculptors could work with the tools of industrial metal casting. The large Lippincott facility could be used to produce sculptures on a scale that was previously impossible for independent artists in the United States.

The sculptor Barnett Newman made his most famous work, *Broken Obelisk*, at Lippincott in 1967. First conceived in 1963, the towering *Broken Obelisk* is based on ancient Egyptian art forms: the pyramid and the obelisk, a tall, four-sided, tapering pillar that ends in a pyramid-like shape at the top. The two shapes are joined point to point; the pyramid acts as a base and the upside-down obelisk, which seems to have been broken in half, juts out from the top. This seemingly impossible connection of classic shapes is made all the more dramatic by the sculpture's color. *Broken Obelisk* is made from a metal alloy called COR-TEN steel, which naturally rusts after several years of exposure to the elements. COR-TEN was a popular choice for monumental sculptures during this period because the rust-red color blends naturally with outdoor settings.

Barnett Newman dedicated his *Broken Obelisk* sculpture (pictured) to slain civil rights leader Martin Luther King Jr. The ragged, broken top edge of the obelisk brings to mind a shattered Washington Monument.

Broken Obelisk has symbolic meaning with roots not only in the vanished ancient Egyptian empire, but in 1960s America. Newman was inspired to create the sculpture after revered civil rights activist Martin Luther King Jr. gave his immortal "I Have a Dream" speech in Washington, DC, in August 1963. As King spoke at the foot of the Lincoln Memorial, the towering obelisk of the Washington Monument glimmered in the distance behind the huge crowd of civil right marchers. After King was assassinated in 1968, Newman dedicated *Broken Obelisk* to him. The move was controversial at the time; during this era of civil unrest, the ragged, broken top edge of the obelisk brought to mind a shattered Washington Monument. As art critic Jonathan Jones explains, "A broken obelisk was a potent emotional way to see America after King's death: the promise denied, the hope shattered, the republic's very rationality snapped in two."[25]

Chicago Picasso

The Lippincott Foundry worked with nearly one hundred well-known sculptors before it closed its doors in 1994. During the time it existed, it produced outdoor works for sculpture gardens, museums, colleges, and city parks throughout the world. However, one of the most famous monumental metal sculptures in the world was not produced at Lippincott. The work, known as *Chicago Picasso*, was molded and fabricated by America's largest steel company, US Steel Corporation in Gary, Indiana.

Chicago Picasso was designed by Pablo Picasso in 1966 when he was eighty-five years old. It was unveiled in 1967 where it stands today, in front of a thirty-one-story steel-and-glass skyscraper on Daley Plaza in downtown Chicago. *Chicago Picasso*, made from COR-TEN steel, resembles a giant bird or winged horse. The sculpture is 50 feet (15.2 m) high and weighs 162 tons (147 metric tons).

Chicago Picasso was controversial when it was first unveiled. Picasso never visited the United States, let alone Chicago, and many viewers were unsettled by the monstrous figure portrayed in steel. But over the years the work became a point of pride in the urban landscape. Like the sculptors of ancient Greece and the Renaissance, Picasso's larger-than-life sculpture transformed the way people viewed the world through the use of fire, metal, and molds.

Chapter Four

The Art of Found Objects

From classical Greece until the impressionist era, sculpture was largely additive, subtractive, or cast in bronze. In 1912 Pablo Picasso singlehandedly changed more than twenty-five hundred years of sculpture tradition when he created *Guitar*. Made from sheet metal and wire, *Guitar* was unlike any other sculpture ever made. It was not carved, modeled, or cast, but cut, folded, stitched, and glued together from separate elements. The work had no base and could not stand on its own. It was hung on the wall for display, neither a flat painting nor a sculptured relief.

Picasso's construction was a new style called assemblage—meaning the sculpture was assembled from various manufactured objects. But *Guitar* was greater than the sum of its pieces, as writer and art critic Guillaume Apollinaire explained in 1913: "[These] strange, coarse, and mismatched materials were ennobled because the artist endowed them with his own delicate and strong personality."[26]

> **Words in Context**
> *assemblage*
> The artistic process of putting together, or assembling, found objects into two- or three-dimensional works of art.

"A Disrupting Visual Shock"

At the time Picasso made *Guitar*, visitors to his studio were often shocked to see his collection of garbage—boxes of empty beer bottles, tin cans, scraps of newspaper, piles of cardboard, and other common objects that no one had ever before attempted to use for artistic purposes. Sometimes Picasso assembled these nonart items into unique sculptures; other times he combined them with paintings and traditional sculpture methods. For example, Picasso made *Glass of Absinthe* (1914) by modeling warm wax with his fingers into a sculpture of a cocktail glass that resembled a human head with disturbingly distorted lips, eyes, and nose. This model was used to make six bronze lost wax casting sculptures, each of which Picasso decorated in a unique fashion, painting the bronze and gluing spoons to the surface.

Picasso also invented a third assemblage element called collage. With collage, pictures are constructed from tangible, identifiable items such as pieces of cloth, newspaper clippings, photos, and other objects. As art professor Sam Hunter writes, Picasso's collage and assemblage sculpture techniques were meant to produce "a disrupting visual shock, since these materials had been snatched from their everyday context."[27]

Words in Context

collage

A technique for producing artwork by assembling various materials, including newspaper clippings, photographs, painted works, and nonart objects such as cloth, coins, and tableware.

"Objects of Formal Beauty"

Picasso's assemblage techniques were quickly adapted by artists in the Dada movement. The Dada style emerged in 1916, during World War I, among European artists who were appalled by the brutality of combat. Dadaists believed that horrific weapons such as tanks, machine guns, and poison gases were the end result of scientific reason and logic. Therefore, they believed the only sane reaction to the barbarism of industrial society was to be irrational and illogical. This led Dadaists to reject carefully created, traditional art in favor of what they called anti-art.

Anti-art was a statement of protest against society and commonly accepted values. Dadaists viewed assemblage sculpture as perfect anti-art because the works were created from rejected objects and pieces of garbage.

Pablo Picasso created a new style of sculpture known as assemblage. These sculptures are created from everyday objects such as bottles, cans, newspaper clippings, cardboard, spoons, and cloth. Pictured is a Picasso assemblage called *Guitar and Bass Bottle* made from pieces of musical instruments.

One of the leading proponents of Dadaism in the United States was Baroness Elsa von Freytag-Loringhoven, a German-born artist who moved to New York City in 1913. The baroness was an eccentric poet and a junk collector who made assemblage sculptures from

Louise Nevelson's Free Expression

Louise Nevelson became one of America's foremost sculptors at an age when most people are thinking about retirement. Her intricate wooden assemblage sculptures made from scavenged materials were not celebrated by critics until 1959, when Nevelson was sixty years old. By that time the sculptor had been an avid member of the New York City arts community for decades.

Born in Kiev, Russia, in 1899, Nevelson emigrated to Rockland, Maine, with her family in 1905. As a child she helped her family make ends meet by selling items she scavenged at a local dump. In 1932 Nevelson enrolled at New York's Art Students League, where she studied painting, sculpture, and printing. Nevelson describes herself during this period as a starving artist who simply lived for her art. By the 1940s Nevelson was creating sculptures with wood and junk that she found in the streets and back alleys of New York.

During this era marked by rigid conformity, Nevelson was a proponent of free expression, which she saw as a political act meant to challenge traditional beliefs. Nevelson carried her belief in free expression into her lifestyle. She wore glamorous gowns, heavy face makeup, and unconventional hairstyles.

Nevelson experienced major success in the early 1960s and continued to create unique sculptures well into her eighties. Her last work, a 35-foot (10.7 m) spiky black steel sculpture called *Sky Horizon,* was installed at the National Institutes of Health in Bethesda, Maryland, just before she died at age eighty-eight on April 17, 1988.

garbage she found in gutters and alleys as well as from items she stole from local stores. Art curator Irene Gammel describes the scene in Freytag-Loringhoven's unheated studio loft around 1917: "Old bits of ironware, automobile tires, gilded [bronze-plated] vegetables, celluloid paintings, ash cans, every conceivable horror, which to her tortured, yet highly sensitized perception, became objects of formal beauty."[28]

With her Dadaist dedication to the bizarre, the baroness used her own body as artwork, as if she were a living sculpture. She was often seen on the streets of New York wearing black lipstick, a purple-and-gold wig, and earrings made from small spoons. She wore a canceled postage stamp on her face, a wooden birdcage hat containing a live canary, and a bra made from tomato cans. This was decades before punk rock made similar fashion statements commonplace; Freytag-Loringhoven evoked fear, laughter, or anger among passersby. She remained unfazed, however. According to Gammel, "With the profound conviction of her own innovative brilliance and against all opposition and ridicule, she insisted that her costumes were art."[29]

The baroness's costumes broke down the boundaries between fashion and art objects; sometimes she incorporated her sculptures directly into her outfits. Her piece called *Limbswish* was an assemblage made of a large metal spring, a cloth curtain tassel, and wire. It resembled a whip, and Freytag-Loringhoven wore it attached to a belt like a cowboy would wear a gun holster. The sculpture referenced the whips her father had sometimes used to inflict harsh discipline upon her during her childhood. In the Dada context the baroness transformed a cruel, punishing object into a work of art that became absurd and even comical as it bounced on her hip.

Shadows and Reflections

With her flamboyant costumes and garbage-picking ways, Freytag-Loringhoven provided inspiration to Louise Nevelson, another European immigrant who turned castoff materials into assemblage sculpture. Nevelson was born in Kiev, Russia, in 1899 and moved to Maine as a child. She learned about the Dada art movement while attending New York's Art Students League in the late 1920s and began making sculptures in the mid-1930s.

Nevelson remained unknown until the mid-1950s, when she first created sculptures from scavenged wooden objects. The assemblages were constructed from street-salvaged remnants of milk crates, boards, spools, table legs, pieces of boats, baseball bats, picture frames, handrail posts, and even toilet seats. Nevelson artfully arranged the scavenged bits of junk wood and stacked them into elegant sculptured walls and room-sized environments. She unified the discarded pieces by painting them a single color, matte black.

In 1959, when Nevelson was sixty years old and had been struggling as an artist for thirty years, she was invited to participate in a show called Sixteen Americans at New York's Museum of Modern Art. The show was so named because it featured the work of sixteen American painters and sculptors. Nevelson constructed a monumental new piece for the show, an assemblage called *Dawn's Wedding Feast*. The sixteen wood assemblage sculptures that made up the piece were gathered into an art installation, a three-dimensional work intended to change how the viewer experiences a particular space. Patrons can walk into such works, where they are surrounded by an environment of artistic sights—and sometimes smells and sounds.

Nevelson had worked only in black at that point, and *Dawn's Wedding Feast* was her first white sculpture. Drawing on inspiration from nineteenth-century impressionists, Nevelson intended to explore areas of dark and light. She explained her transformation from black to white: "[Before] I wanted simply to give structure to shadow; now I want to give structure and permanence to reflection."[30] To viewers the white reflections represented bright prospects, serenity, and joy.

The sculptures of *Dawn's Wedding Feast* represented a bride and groom surrounded by guests that were symbolized by standing and hanging columns. Sculptures representing a wedding chest, pillows, and cake were placed around the installation. The pieces were enclosed by large wall-sized ensembles suggesting interiors of a wedding chapel. With separate sculptures brought together into a single installation, *Dawn's Wedding Feast* represented the joining of a woman, a man, and their families through marriage.

Nevelson's installation was favorably received by critics and viewers alike and helped her gain widespread recognition as a sculptor. In the years that followed, Nevelson's work expanded to heroic proportions. The haunting 1964 Holocaust memorial, *Homage to 6,000,000 I*, stretched 225 feet (68.6 m). The somber sculpture is constructed from dozens of wooden boxes filled with collections of personal items, all painted black. No two boxes are alike. They are meant to represent intimate portraits of the individual Jewish people who were among the anonymous millions killed during the Holocaust.

"The Stuff of Life and the Stuff of Art"

Like Nevelson, artist Robert Rauschenberg participated in Sixteen Americans, and as with Nevelson, the show helped him reach a wide audience. Although Nevelson mainly worked with found wooden objects, Rauschenberg expanded the assemblage palette to include nearly anything and everything.

Born in Port Arthur, Texas, in 1925, Rauschenberg moved to New York City in 1949. After experimenting with photography and painting, he began making works he called "elemental sculptures" in 1953. The works featured what were considered unusual materials, including stones, rope, rusted bolts and nails, and weathered wood. Rauschenberg referred to some of the elemental sculptures as "dirt paintings." These works were made from clay and earth arranged in shallow wooden boxes. When the grass seeds in one dirt painting sprouted into living plants, Rauschenberg visited the gallery where they were displayed to water them.

Despite his unique viewpoint, Rauschenberg earned little with his artistic experiments. In 1954, unable to afford expensive art materials, Rauschenberg began collecting an astonishing array of discarded objects he found in abundance in his run-down New York neighborhood. The materials included half-empty cans of house paint, crates, cloth, used signs, photographs, old magazines, machine parts, abandoned furniture, plumbing fixtures, mirrors, cork, rubber tires, and soda bottles. A neighborhood taxidermist provided Rauschenberg with preserved animals, including an Angora goat, a chicken, and a bald eagle.

Rauschenberg used the found items to create what he called "combines," combinations of painting, collage, and sculpture. The sculptures were meant to encapsulate the artist's life, his personal feelings and emotions, and his surroundings in the urban environment.

American artist Robert Rauschenberg often used discarded objects including signs, crates, machine parts, old magazines, and tires to create his sculptures. This Rauschenberg sculpture is one of several exhibited at a museum in Switzerland.

One of Rauschenberg's first combines, *Untitled* (1954), is constructed from several box-like pieces mounted on furniture wheels called casters. The work incorporates photographs of the artist's ex-wife, newspaper clippings about his parents from a hometown paper, and a sentimental letter from his young son. Random photos clipped from magazines, such as a woman kissing her young daughter and a man crying in anguish, provide an emotional element to the piece. A pair of painted leather shoes is meant to evoke feelings of loneliness or abandonment. The intimate elements of the piece act almost as a scrapbook or diary of Rauschenberg's life. *Untitled* also contains some humorous elements; a stuffed Dominique hen is posed next to and stands in contrast with an elegant man dressed in a white suit. Art critic Michael Kimmelman comments on Rauschenberg's use of materials: "It is largely, if not exclusively, thanks to Robert Rauschenberg that Americans since the 1950's have come to think that art can be made out of anything, exist anywhere, last forever or just for a moment and serve almost any purpose or no purpose at all except to suggest that the stuff of life and the stuff of art are ultimately one and the same."[31]

"Stupid as Life Itself"

While Rauschenberg incorporated everyday objects into his combines, Claes Oldenburg used common items as models to create large sculptures. Born in Sweden in 1929, Oldenburg moved to Chicago with his parents at age six. By the mid-1960s he was famous for inventing "soft sculptures," large sagging pieces fashioned from vinyl, foam rubber, plastic tubing, and Plexiglas.

Oldenburg's 1963 soft sculpture *Giant BLT (Bacon, Lettuce and Tomato Sandwich)* is 39 inches (99 cm) long and 29 inches (74 cm) high. The brightly colored, multilayered vinyl sandwich, hand sewed by Oldenburg's first wife, Pat Oldenburg, features a toothpick through the middle and an olive on top.

Other soft sculptures included an oversized hamburger, a slice of cake, an ice-cream cone, a fan, a washstand, a toilet, gym shoes, and lingerie. These works were inspired by Oldenburg's fascination with the stuff of everyday life. To draw attention to the shapes and sizes of commonplace things, he made hard objects soft and small items large, and he exaggerated their features. As Oldenburg wrote in a 1961 poem, "I am for an art that takes its form from the lines of life itself, that twists and extends

> **Words in Context**
> *Plexiglas*
> The trade name of a tough, transparent acrylic plastic that is often used in place of glass.

and accumulates and spits and drips, and is heavy and coarse and blunt and sweet and stupid as life itself."[32]

Oldenburg's sculptures are classified as popular or pop art, a form that emerged in the 1960s as a reaction to consumer culture. Pop artists believed that a person's reality in the second half of the twentieth century was not shaped by the natural world but by advertising, consumption, and manufactured goods. Items such as fast food, appliances, and cars, according to this logic, were not necessarily marketed for their utility but for the ability to provide happiness and in some cases make dreams come true.

The artist who personified pop art, Andy Warhol, achieved widespread fame for his paintings of soup cans and soap boxes, products so common at the time they were in nearly every American household. Even though Warhol and Oldenburg were slyly mocking consumer culture, their work was popular because it had broad appeal. Average viewers understood soup cans and giant BLTs, while works by Dadaists earlier in the century were largely beyond public comprehension.

Comically Large Objects

In 1976 Oldenburg began collaborating with Dutch American pop sculptor Coosje van Bruggen, and the couple married the following year. Oldenburg and van Bruggen exploded the scale of common objects and created comically large, one-of-a-kind sculptures that were displayed throughout the world. Their first collaboration, *Trowel I* (1976), is a steel garden trowel nearly 42 feet (12.8 m) high, placed in a garden park in Netherlands. It is painted bright blue, like a Dutch workman's overalls, and stands with the pointed edge dug down into the dirt.

Oldenburg and van Bruggen created more than forty large-scale public sculptures between 1976 and 2009. They are modeled on pool balls, a flashlight, cowboy hats, a toothbrush, a knife that appears to be cutting through a building, and a dropped bowl with scattered orange slices and peels. Perhaps the most famous work, *Spoonbridge and Cherry* (1988), consists of a giant steel spoon holding a bright red cherry.

Spoonbridge and Cherry, a giant sculpture by Claes Oldenburg and Coosje van Bruggen, arches over a pond in the Walker Art Center sculpture garden in Minneapolis, Minnesota. The playful sculpture beckons onlookers in both winter and summer.

Displayed in a sculpture garden at Walker Art Center in Minneapolis, *Spoonbridge and Cherry* is a massive piece of tableware that arches over a pond. The upturned bowl of the spoon rests on an island and holds a cherry with a long stem. *Spoonbridge and Cherry* stretches more than 51 feet (15.5 m), is 29 feet (8.8 m) high, and weighs 7,000 pounds (3,175 kg). Despite its scale, the sculpture appears light and does not overwhelm the other forty sculptures in the garden.

Oldenburg and van Bruggen designed *Spoonbridge and Cherry* to appear inviting in both the warm months and the long, cold Minneapolis winters. In the summer the stem is a water fountain that coats the bright red cherry in a glistening sparkle that makes it appear almost edible. In the winter the cherry is topped with snow, which gives it the appearance of an ice-cream sundae.

Installation Art Happenings

Artists create installations to exhibit a variety of media that may include painting, sculpture, photographs, videos, music, poetry, and live performance. Patrons visiting an installation enter a room or space and wander between different aspects of an artistic environment. Unlike the calm and quiet layout of a traditional art museum, an art installation may be filled with dissimilar combinations of sculpture, painting, and nonart materials. Rather than create harmony, the contrasting pieces are meant to evoke complex emotions such as puzzlement, longing, wistfulness, sadness, elation, or even anger.

The first installations were created in 1959 by American painter, performer, and conceptual artist Allan Kaprow, who invented what are now called art happenings. Happenings were singular events that featured music, photography, dance, poetry readings, paintings, light shows, and sculptures. Kaprow thought New York's expensive, white-walled galleries were sterile and uninspiring. Rather than host happenings at these boring venues, Kaprow held the happenings in empty lots, dirty lofts, closed shops, and abandoned buildings.

For his 1960 happening, *Apple Shrine*, Kaprow filled a long, narrow room in a church basement with assemblages of tangled chicken wire, colored lights, crumpled newspapers, straw, cloth, fake and real apples, and reeking piles of garbage. Kaprow created the installation to draw attention to everyday environments people generally ignored. His happenings drew large audiences that included sculptors Robert Rauschenberg, Louise Nevelson, and Claes Oldenburg. Because of Kaprow's unique vision, art installations since the 1960s have redefined art, the artist, and the exhibition space.

While not assembled from dozens of everyday objects, *Spoon-bridge and Cherry* and other Oldenburg and van Bruggen sculptures portray singular items. And like Picasso's *Guitar* the sculptures embody the clever humor and oversized personalities of the sculptors even as they provide a different perspective on everyday life. As Rauschenberg biographer Catherine Craft explains, the sculptures "[give] us the possibility of seeing anew objects and images that we tend to overlook in our daily lives."[33]

Chapter Five

Concepts in Sculpture

In 1915 the twenty-eight-year old French artist Marcel Duchamp was living in New York City when he began collecting manufactured objects, including a snow shovel, a dog grooming comb, and a typewriter case. Within a few years Duchamp was displaying these items as works of art. Duchamp coined the term *readymade* to define a purchased object he considered "a sculpture already made."[34]

Today Duchamp is among the most well-known sculptors of the twentieth century, but he began his career as a cubist painter. His 1912 painting *Nude Descending a Staircase No. 2* portrays an abstract figure that seems to move across the canvas in a series of overlapping, violently jagged images.

Nude Descending a Staircase No. 2 is now considered an innovative masterpiece. However, when the painting was initially exhibited, at the 1913 Armory Show in New York City, Americans were scandalized. At the time people in the United States had had little exposure to European cubism, and critics were merciless. The figure in the painting was compared to a bag of golf clubs, a stairway in ruins after an earthquake, and a bunch of broken violins. *New York Times* art critic Julian Street wrote that *Nude Descending a Staircase No. 2* looked like "an explosion in a shingle factory."[35]

A Bike Wheel as Sculpture

After the Armory Show, Duchamp had had his fill of painting and art critics. While viewing airplanes at an aviation exhibition,

Duchamp realized there was great beauty in mechanical objects. He told Romanian sculptor Constantin Brancusi, "Painting's washed up. Who'll do anything better than that [airplane] propeller?"[36]

After the Armory Show, Duchamp set out to transform nonart into sculpture. He took the front fork of a bicycle, complete with its spoke wheel, and mounted it upside down on a wooden stool. *Bicycle Wheel* combined several readymades into a single sculpture, so Duchamp called it an assisted readymade. Duchamp appreciated *Bicycle Wheel* as a soothing distraction that attracted his gaze as he worked.

Words in Context
readymade
A manufactured object, such as a bicycle wheel or snow shovel, displayed as a work of art.

As he later wrote, "To set the wheel turning was very soothing, very comforting. . . . I liked the idea of having a bicycle wheel in my studio. I enjoyed looking at it, just as I enjoyed looking at the flames dancing in a fireplace."[37]

Mr. Mutt's *Fountain*

The concept of turning a bicycle wheel into a sculpture would not have advanced the careers of most artists. However, the stinging reviews of *Nude Descending a Staircase No. 2* made Duchamp famous within New York art circles. This led him to make friends with Dada artist Man Ray and wealthy art patrons Louise and Walter Conrad Arensberg. The Arensbergs provided Duchamp with a studio and paid him $10,000 a year, a large sum at the time, in exchange for any artwork he might produce. However, by this time Duchamp was not interested in producing art that evoked any sort of emotion. Instead he wanted to find art objects that were neither beautiful nor ugly, but unexceptional. These objects projected what Duchamp called "visual indifference."[38]

In 1917, during a search for visually indifferent objects, Duchamp visited the plumbing supply store J.L. Mott Iron Works on New York's Fifth Avenue. He purchased a white porcelain urinal, took it to his studio, and mounted it flat on its back. Duchamp signed the work "R. Mutt, 1917," a play on words since J.L. Mott was where the urinal was purchased.

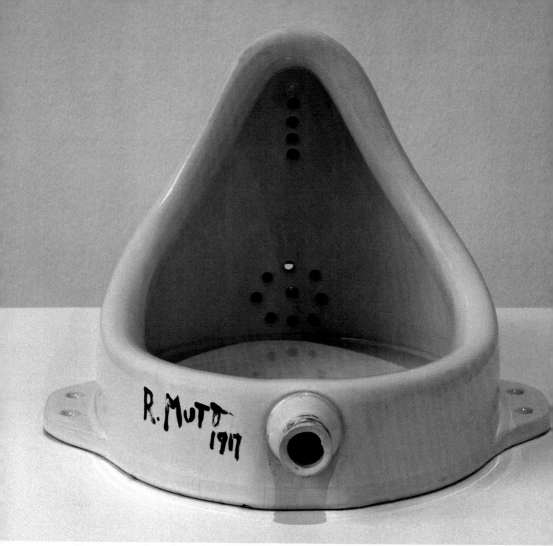

Curators refused to display Marcel Duchamp's *Fountain* (pictured) at the first annual exhibition of the Society of Independent Artists in New York. Some thought the work was vulgar while others simply did not consider the signed and dated porcelain urinal to be art.

Duchamp entered *Fountain* under the pseudonym R. Mutt in the first annual exhibition of the Society of Independent Artists at New York's Grand Central Palace. Although he used the pseudonym R. Mutt, Duchamp was a board member of the society, and it was common knowledge that *Fountain* was his submission. The society's policy was to display any artwork submitted, but the group's curators refused to put *Fountain* in the show. Some thought the work was vulgar and immoral, while others simply did not consider the plumbing fixture worthy of an art exhibit.

While *Fountain* never displayed at the Society of Independent Artists show, Duchamp arranged to have it photographed by Alfred Stieglitz, one of the era's most successful photographers. A single photograph is the only record of *Fountain*; Stieglitz threw the work away after the picture was taken. However, the photograph was printed in the Dada magazine *Blind Man* along with Duchamp's defense of his readymade:

> Now Mr. Mutt's fountain is not immoral, that is absurd. . . . It is a fixture which you see every day in plumbers' show windows. Whether Mr. Mutt made the fountain with his own hands or not has no importance. He CHOSE it. He took an article of life, placed it so that its useful significance disappeared under the new title and point of view—created a new thought for that object. As for plumbing, that is absurd. The only works of art America has produced are her plumbing and her bridges.[39]

Fountain quickly became a symbol of the Dada movement. The fact that a common plumbing appliance could generate such astonishment reinforced the Dada philosophy—society appeared ridiculous, more so than the artist who displayed the fixture as sculpture.

Duchamp might have had a playful intent when he created *Fountain* and his other readymades, but he was seriously challenging basic concepts of art. For thousands of years sculptors had been admired for their uncommon talent and skill. When Duchamp displayed a urinal in an art show, it was a work of spontaneous creation rather than extended planning. With *Fountain* Duchamp announced that anything could be a sculpture if it was signed by an artist or displayed as art.

The Concept of Art

Duchamp's intent mattered little in the press. Critics expressed shock and indignation—and printed the Stieglitz photograph dozens of times. By this time everyone knew R. Mutt was Marcel Duchamp, and just as the artist had planned, the publicity brought him widespread fame. And the readymade had staying power. In 2004 *Fountain* was voted one of the most influential sculptures of the twentieth century in a poll of five hundred British art scholars and professionals. British art critic Philip Hensher explained the importance of *Fountain*: "With this single 'readymade' work, Duchamp invented conceptual art and severed forever the traditional link between the artist's labor and the merit of the work."[40]

While Duchamp might have invented conceptual art, the term was not widely used until anti-artist Henry Flynt coined the term *concept art* in 1961. According to Flynt, the thought or concept of an artwork was more important than the materials used to make it: "Concept art [is] an art of which the material is *concepts*, as the material of . . . music is sound. Since concepts are closely bound up with language, concept art is a kind of art of which the material is language."[41] In simpler terms, art is whatever the artist says it is.

> **Words in Context**
> *conceptual art*
> Work in which the idea, or concept, of the art is more important than the actual materials or execution. With conceptual art, the planning takes place before display, and the actual creation of the piece is fast and simple.

Around the time of Flynt's declaration, the Bulgarian-born artist Christo Javacheff and his French wife Jeanne-Claude, with whom he lived in Paris, decided that large metal barrels used to hold oil were art. They collected dozens of used barrels from a local junkyard and carried them up to their seventh-floor art studio. After the barrels were cleaned, Christo and Jeanne-Claude wrapped them in fabric, rope, wire mesh, and other materials. They believed that by concealing the everyday objects, they were better able to draw attention to them. By June 1962 the couple had eighty-nine wrapped oil barrels that they decided to assemble into a sculpture that could not be ignored.

Christo and Jeanne-Claude illegally stacked the oil barrels to create a wall blocking Rue Visconti, a narrow but busy street near their studio. The work was called *Iron Curtain*. At the time the term *iron curtain* symbolized the repressive Communist authority the Soviet Union exerted over Eastern Europe after World War II, including Christo's native Bulgaria. One of the most potent symbols of the iron curtain was the Berlin Wall, a militarized concrete barrier the Soviets

Man Ray and His Readymades

When Marcel Duchamp began creating readymade sculptures in New York City in 1915, one of his closest collaborators was the Brooklyn-born artist Man Ray. Duchamp introduced Ray to an elite group of writers and artists, including Pablo Picasso, Ernest Hemingway, and Salvador Dali. Ray began taking photos of the celebrities, and his commercial success allowed him to experiment with photography. By 1920 Ray was one of the leading photographers in the Dada movement.

Inspired by his friend Duchamp, Ray also created readymades. Ray's *The Gift* (1921) is a sculpture that incorporated found objects; he glued long brass tacks to the surface of a clothing iron. Another Ray readymade, *Object to Be Destroyed* (1923), is a metronome, a time-keeping device used by musicians. Ray attached an enlarged photograph of a woman's eye to the swinging arm of the metronome. As the eye moved back and forth, the object gave viewers a disturbing feeling of being watched while evoking feelings of helplessness in the face of endless time.

Ray also incorporated found objects into his unique photos he called Rayographs. Ray created the Rayographs by placing objects such keys, wire mesh, paper scraps, and even a pistol on sheets of unexposed photographic print paper. When exposed to short bursts of light, the objects made silhouettes on the paper. In the 1950s Ray concentrated on painting and sculpture and wrote an autobiography titled *Self Portrait*. He died in Paris in 1976 at age eighty-eight.

constructed across the German city of Berlin in August 1961. The Berlin Wall prevented citizens of Communist Eastern Europe from migrating to democratic Western Europe. Christo had recently escaped from Bulgaria and wanted to draw attention to the control the Soviets imposed upon movement.

The *Iron Curtain* stood across Rue Visconti for eight hours and created a massive traffic jam that inconvenienced thousands of people. Christo later joked that the conceptual artwork was not the eighty-nine oil barrels but the traffic jam itself.

Wrapping Objects

By 1964 Christo and Jeanne-Claude were constantly creating wrapped sculptures. They wound fabric, polyethylene (plastic) sheets, rope, and twine around an ancient Roman garden sculpture, a Vespa motorbike, and a 1963 Volkswagen Beetle. They even (temporarily) wrapped a woman who volunteered as a model. Art critic Adam Thomas Blackbourn explains the wrapping concept:

> Christo's *Wrapped Objects* explore the transformative effect fabric and tactile surfaces have when wrapped around familiar objects. The concealment caused by the fabric challenges the viewer to reappraise the objects beneath and the space in which it exists. For those *Wrapped Objects* that are packaged in translucent polyethylene, little is left to the imagination, but the material gives the everyday objects an additional sculptural quality.[42]

After wrapping most of the contents of their studio, Christo and Jeanne-Claude decided to turn entire buildings into sculptures worthy of artistic consideration and study. In 1968 they created the first of what they called temporary monuments, wrapping an entire three-story medieval tower in Spoleto, Italy, with woven polypropylene fabric and ropes. The following year the pair turned the Museum of Contemporary Art in Chicago into a temporary monument of epic proportions. They wrapped the massive museum in a 10,000-square-foot (929 sq. m) greenish-brown tarpaulin held in place with 4,000 feet (1,219 m) of Manila rope.

Christo and Jeanne-Claude believed the dull-looking one-story building was perfect for wrapping since it already resembled an anonymous brown package. The project was undertaken in the winter, and the dark tarp stood in stark contrast to the snow piled up on the city

Workers wrap trees in a Swiss park, one of the many examples of *Wrapped Objects* by artists Christo and Jeanne-Claude. Their wrapped sculptures have included a sculpture garden, a Volkswagen Beetle, and whole buildings.

streets. The tightly tied cloth also gave the appearance of a building bundled up against the cold and blustery Chicago wind.

Environmental Artists

In 1968 Christo and Jeanne-Claude rejected the term *conceptual art* and labeled themselves environmental artists. Rather than give new form to urban structures, the couple now wished to draw attention to distance and dimension in the natural world. They did so by transforming various landscapes into massive cloth sculptures that stretched for miles.

The first environmental project, *Wrapped Coast*, was installed in Little Bay, along the Pacific coast near Sydney, Australia. With the help of a workforce of 15 professional mountain climbers and 110 art and architectural students from local colleges, the rocky coastal cliffs

Environmental Sculptures

Beth Galston is a leading environmental sculptor who creates natural artwork for interior and exterior display. She explores various aspects of environmental sculpture on her website:

An environmental sculpture has a special relationship with its surroundings. It's planned for a particular site, and the qualities of that site influence the making of the artwork. The space can be anywhere— a room, a grove of trees, a pond, an alleyway, a public plaza, a complex of buildings. Often existing on a grand scale, an environmental sculpture surrounds its viewers, who experience the artwork as they enter and move through the space. The elements of time and movement, then, are also involved as important parts of the viewer's experience. . . .

[Environmental] sculpture is an artwork that's inspired by forms and processes from nature. Many artists use materials, shapes, colors and textures from the natural environment. Others explore meanings of natural cycles, such as the four seasons; metamorphosis; cycles of birth, growth, aging, death, and decay. Natural processes are used as metaphors to reflect on the passage of time, capture a fleeting moment, express a sense of loss, or a hope for regeneration. Some environmental artists use ecological issues as their subject matter, and their work seeks to heighten awareness of a fragile ecology, or even to reclaim land, such as by using plant materials to alleviate pollution problems, returning an area to a more pristine condition.

Beth Galston, "Thoughts on Environmental Sculpture," Beth Galston Sculptor, 2013. www.bethgalston.com.

were draped with 1.5 miles (2.4 km) of light beige plastic fabric 150 to 800 feet (46 m to 244 m) wide. The fabric was held in place by 35 miles (56.3 km) of polypropylene rope.

Visitors to the *Wrapped Coast* experienced the odd sensation of walking near the ocean while stepping on soft, fabric-covered ground that made a slight crunching sound under their feet. As the weather changed and the sun rose and set, the tone and color of the sculpture reflected almost unearthly hues. Some compared the synthetic landscape to something from a science-fiction film or the surface of the moon.

Wrapped Coast was displayed for ten weeks beginning in late October 1968, after which all materials were removed and recycled. During its short life, the sculpture helped place nature in a new context for the thousands of visitors who came to view the work.

The Art of People, Places, and Events

Wrapped Coast brought widespread recognition to Christo and Jeanne-Claude, and their projects grew in scope as their fame increased. In September 1976 the couple completed *Running Fence*. The sculpture stretched 24.5 miles (39.4 km) across Northern California, through Sonoma and Marin Counties down to the Pacific Ocean at Bodega Bay. Built from more than 2.1 million square feet (195,096 sq. m) of white fabric, the sculpture was 18 feet (5.5 m) high. It was hung from steel cables attached to 2,050 tall steel poles, each embedded 3 feet (91.4 cm) into the ground.

Running Fence crossed fourteen roads, and the artists left space for cars, cattle, and wildlife to cross. The sculpture also crossed fields owned by more than twenty ranchers, who granted permission to Christo and Jeanne-Claude to use their land. The entire project took forty-two months to construct; the artists were required to draft an environmental impact statement and attend eighteen public meetings in order to obtain official government permits. However, *Running Fence* existed for only two weeks. In this way the fence was only one element of the total sculpture project. The art of *Running Fence* included the effect it had on the hundreds of people whose lives it touched. The Smithsonian American Art Museum website explains, "The story of *Running Fence* is not only a story of the inexhaustible perseverance of two artists over nearly insurmountable odds to create a temporary artwork of joy and beauty, but also the story of the people, places, and events that would become what is known as *Running Fence*."[43]

The Gates Shimmy like Dancers

With the completion of the California project, the environmental projects by Christo and Jeanne-Claude came to be known as Christos. Despite their growing fame, the artists continually struggled to create new projects. They refused to accept commercial sponsors and self-financed all their environmental sculptures through the sale of drawings, collages, and scale models. The couple also waged long, costly battles against bureaucratic opposition; it took the artists twenty-six years to obtain permission to construct *The Gates* in New York's Central Park. The project featured 7,503 saffron (bright orange) fabric pan-

Among the most ambitious sculptures created by Christo and Jeanne-Claude is *The Gates*, a series of 7,503 bright orange fabric panels on 16-foot-high metal frames located in New York's Central Park. The brightly colored cloth panels provided a sharp contrast with the park's leafless trees in winter.

els on 16-foot-high (4.9 m) metal frames. Putting it together required Christo and Jeanne-Claude to attend countless zoning board hearings, public forums, government debates, public and private meetings, legal and contract negotiations, and press conferences.

The Gates was finally finished on a snowy day in February 2005 and was in place for sixteen days. The gates were of twenty-five different widths, from 5 feet 6 inches (1.7 m) to 18 feet (5.5 m). They were built along 23 miles (37 km) of sidewalk in Central Park. The saffron swaths of pleated nylon provided a sharp contrast to the park's leafless trees and piles of white snow. *New York Times* architecture critic Michael Kimmelman described the artistic effect of the sculpture:

> In the winter light, the bright fabric seemed to warm the fields, flickering like a flame against the barren trees. Even at first blush, it was clear that "The Gates" is a work of pure joy, a vast populist spectacle of good will and simple eloquence, the first great public art event of the 21st century. . . . Sometimes the fabric looked deep orange; at other times it was shiny, like gold leaf, or silvery or almost tan. In the breeze, the skirted gates also appeared to shimmy like dancers in a conga line, the cloth buckling and swaying.[44]

Land Art

The Gates and other Christos changed the appearance of the environment. But some conceptual sculptures are themselves made from the environment and are part of the natural world. These conceptual sculptures, formed from dirt, rocks, wood, water, and plants, are meant to break down the boundaries between nature and art.

Words in Context
geoglyph
A large design produced on the ground, usually formed from local natural materials such as rocks, dirt, stones, and live trees.

Australian sculptor Andrew Rogers calls his environmental concepts land art. His Rhythms of Life series was an incredibly ambitious undertaking that grew into the largest environmental art project in the world. It consists of forty-eight huge geoglyphs—large sculptures made from rocks, stone, gravel, and live trees. These sculptures of horses, llamas, columns, arcs, and flowing natural shapes are similar to those built by ancient tribes thousands of years ago in Peru and elsewhere.

Rogers started the Rhythms of Life project in 1998 and in the fourteen years that followed constructed sculptures in thirteen countries on all seven continents. Rogers traveled to India, the Middle East, Africa, the United States, and Europe to create symbols that had meaning among the local people. Many residents volunteered to create the sculptures on hillsides, mountaintops, plains, and in valleys. Some are on such a grand scale they can best be appreciated from a helicopter—or from satellite photos posted on the Internet.

The 5-foot-high (1.5 m) sculpture *Shield* in Chyulu Hills, Kenya, for example, stretches over an area 328 by 230 feet (100 m by 70 m). It depicts two symbols, a giant shield and a lion's paw. Both figures represent strength, tradition, and endurance to the nomadic Maasai people who live in the region. Rogers recruited 1,270 Maasai volunteers, who carried local stones to the site and placed them along GPS coordinates worked out by Rogers.

Rogers considers *Shield* a gift to the next Maasai generation, but the sculpture will disappear over time. When the walls collapse, the materials will be absorbed back into the earth. Like the shifting tides and the changing seasons, environmental art is temporary art that exists in time as well as place.

Joy of Creation

Rogers's land art sculptures were built by more than sixty-seven hundred volunteers. With their roots in ancient cultures, the sculptures are unlike the manufactured goods displayed by Duchamp or Christo and Jeanne-Claude. Land art is not made in a factory but through the labor of people who found joy through a work of beauty.

What readymades, conceptual sculptures, and land art do have in common, however, is the ability to evoke emotions. While Duchamp wished to shock, the billowing fabric of the Christos and the geoglyphs of Rogers bring happiness. And moving viewers to sadness, awe, affection, and a range of other feelings has been the job of the sculptor since the first clay figurines were made more than thirty thousand years ago.

Source Notes

Introduction: What Is the Art of Sculpture?

1. Martin Bailey, "Ice Age Lion Man Is World's Earliest Figurative Sculpture," *Art Newspaper*, January 31, 2013. www.theart newspaper.com.

Chapter One: Bringing Clay to Life

2. Quoted in Travel China Guide, "Qin Terra Cotta Artisans," 2013. www.travelchinaguide.com.

3. Quoted in Shim Chung, "The Monstrous and the Grotesque: Gauguin's Ceramic Sculpture," *Image & Narrative*, November 2008. www.imageandnarrative.be.

4. Quoted in Chung, "The Monstrous and the Grotesque."

5. Quoted in Musée d'Orsay, "Paul Gauguin: *Oviri*," 2006. www .musee-orsay.fr/en.

6. Quoted in Musée d'Orsay, "Paul Gauguin: *Oviri*."

7. John Blee, "Paradise and Modernism: Gauguin at the National Gallery," *Georgetowner* (Washington, DC), March 8, 2011. www.georgetowner.com.

8. Quoted in Lael Wertenbaker, *The World of Picasso*. Alexandria, VA: Time-Life, 1966, p. 149.

Chapter Two: Inspiration in Stone

9. Quoted in Elizabeth Prettejohn, *The Modernity of Ancient Sculpture*. London: Tauris, 2012, p. 13.

10. Quoted in James Daly, "Up Front: The Angel in the Marble," *Edutopia*, October 9, 2013. www.edutopia.org.

11. Hans Koepf, *Masterpieces of Sculpture*. New York: Putnam, 1961, p. 18.

12. Quoted in Vincent Finnan, "Michelangelo *David*," Italian Renaissance Art.com, 2013. www.italian-renaissance-art.com.

13. Quoted in Mark Callaghan, "Michelangelo's *David*," *Italy Magazine*, September 9, 2009. www.italymagazine.com.

14. Sheldon Cheney, *Sculpture of the World: A History*. New York: Viking, 1968, pp. 366–67.

15. Grace Glueck, "Rodin and Michelangelo, Together at Last," *New York Times*, April 18, 1997. www.nytimes.com.

16. Quoted in Rex Alan Smith, *The Carving of Mount Rushmore*. New York: Abbeville, 1985, p. 21.

17. Quoted in Garden of Praise, "Gutzon Borglum," 2013. http://gardenofpraise.com.

Chapter Three: Beauty in Bronze

18. Quoted in George Willis Botsford and E.G. Sihler, eds., *Hellenic Civilization*. New York: Columbia University Press, 1915, pp. 549–50.

19. Christian Hauser, *Art Foundry*. New York: Van Nostrand Reinhold, 1972, pp. 11–12.

20. Giorgio Vasari, *Stories of the Italian Artists from Vasari*, trans. E.L. Seely. New York: Duffield, 1907, p. 77.

21. Bruce Cole, *Masaccio and the Art of Early Renaissance Florence*. Bloomington: Indiana University Press, 1980, p. 94.

22. Quoted in David Ekserdjian, ed., *Bronze*. London: Royal Academy of the Arts, 2012, p. 94.

23. Quoted in Ekserdjian, *Bronze*, p. 95.

24. Musée Rodin, "The Thinker," 2013. www.musee-rodin.fr.

25. Jonathan Jones, "Newman's Broken Obelisk: The End of a Political Dream," *Guardian* (London), October 22, 2008. www.theguardian.com.

Chapter Four: The Art of Found Objects

26. Quoted in MoMA, "Picasso Guitars, 1912–1914," 2011. www.moma.org.

27. Sam Hunter, *Picasso: Cubism and After*. New York: Abrams, 1969, p. 12.

28. Irene Gammel, *Baroness Elsa*. Cambridge, MA: MIT Press, 2002, p. 220.

29. Gammel, *Baroness Elsa*, p. 185.

30. Quoted in Bernard Ceysson et al., *Sculpture from the Renaissance to the Present Day*. New York: Taschen, 1996, p. 527.

31. Michael Kimmelman, "Art out of Anything: Rauschenberg in Retrospect," *New York Times*, December 23, 2005. www.nytimes.com.

32. Quoted in Ceysson, *Sculpture from the Renaissance to the Present Day*, p. 535.

33. Catherine Craft, *Robert Rauschenberg*. London: Phaidon Press, 2013, p. 5.

Chapter 5: Concepts in Sculpture

34. Quoted in MoMA, "The Collection," 2013. www.moma.org.

35. Quoted in Milton W. Brown, *The Story of the Armory Show*. New York: Abbeville, 1988, p. 137.

36. Quoted in Catherine Craft, *An Audience of Artists: Dada, Neo-Dada, and the Emergence of Abstract Expressionism*. Chicago: University of Chicago Press, 2012, p. 28.

37. Quoted in Toutfait, "Bicycle Wheel," 2013. www.toutfait.com.

38. Quoted in Martha Buskirk and Mignon Nixon, eds., *The Duchamp Effect*. Cambridge, MA: MIT Press, 1996, p. 104.

39. Quoted in Juan Antonio Ramirez, *Duchamp: Love and Death, Even*. London: Reaktion, 1999, p. 54.

40. Philip Hensher, "The Loo That Shook the World: Duchamp, Man Ray, Picabi," *Independent* (London), February 20, 2008. www .independent.co.uk.

41. Quoted in Radical Art, "Henry Flynt Concept Art," 2007. http:// radicalart.info.

42. Adam Thomas Blackbourn, "Wrapped Objects, Statues and Women," Christo and Jeanne-Claude, 2011. www.christojean neclaude.net.

43. Smithsonian American Art Museum, "Christo and Jeanne-Claude: Remembering the Running Fence," 2010. http://ameri canart.si.edu/exhibitions/archive/2010/christo.

44. Michael Kimmelman, "In a Saffron Ribbon, a Billowy Gift to the City," *New York Times*, February 13, 2005. www.nytimes.com.

Books

Phyllis Raybin Emert, *Michelangelo*. Farmington Hills, MI: Greenhaven, 2012.

Jacky Klein and Suzy Klein, *What Is Contemporary Art?* New York: Museum of Modern Art, 2012.

Don Nardo, *Ancient Egyptian Art and Architecture*. Farmington Hills, MI: Lucent, 2011.

Emma J. Stafford, *Exploring the Life, Myth, and Art of Ancient Greece*. New York: Rosen, 2011.

Gary van Wyk, *Pop Art: 50 Works of Art You Should Know*. New York: Prestel, 2013.

Websites

Andrew Rogers (www.andrewrogers.org). This site features photos and videos of Rogers's one-of-a-kind Rhythms of Life land art project. The project consists of forty-eight structures in thirteen countries, from Antarctica to Sri Lanka and the United States.

Artble (www.artble.com). This website features hundreds of the world's most famous artworks, the stories behind their creation, artistic analysis, and critical reception of pieces when they were first exhibited. Pages on Donatello, Rodin, and others feature in-depth explorations of their sculptural masterpieces.

Christo and Jeanne-Claude (www.christojeanneclaude.net). The home page of the husband-and-wife team of conceptual artists famous for wrapping large buildings and natural sites in plastic and canvas. The couple's many projects from 1958 until the twenty-first century are discussed, and many photos are provided.

Lippincott Sculptural Fabrication and Conservation (www.lippincottsculpture.com). Lippincott was a fine-arts metal foundry and metal fabricating company that created large-scale sculptures for the world's most famous sculptors, including Keith Haring, Claes Oldenburg, and Barnett Newman. This site features photos of the foundry's work, company history, and links to artist pages.

Louise Nevelson Foundation (www.louisenevelsonfoundation.org). This site is home to one of the twentieth century's most well-known assemblage sculptors and features biographical information, educational programs, and media displaying Nevelson's large body of work.

Marcel Duchamp World Community (www.marcelduchamp.net). This website provides art reproductions, essays, interviews, and biographical and exhibition information concerning the man whose readymades and conceptual art provided the foundation for twentieth-century sculpture.

Museum of Modern Art (MoMA) (www.moma.com). This site covers some of the world's most famous artists and art movements of the past 120 years, with photos, videos, historical information, educational podcasts, lectures, and commentary.

On-Line Picasso Project (https://picasso.shsu.edu). A comprehensive illustrated catalog with links to more than twelve thousand paintings, four thousand articles, and thousands of commentaries and notes concerning Picasso's entire body of work broken down by year.

Robert Rauschenberg Foundation (www.rauschenbergfoundation.org). The Rauschenberg Foundation offers grants and artist programs and delves into the artist's legacy with biographical information, a video archive, and a catalog of works and exhibitions.

Index